To Honolulu in Five Days

TO HONOLULU IN FIVE DAYS

FIVE DAYS

Cruising Aboard Matson's S.S. *Lurline*

Lynn Blocker Krantz, Nick Krantz, and Mary Thiele Fobian

TEN SPEED PRESS

Berkeley / Toronto

Ten Speed Press
PO Box 7123
Berkeley, California 94707

Distributed in Australia by Simon and Schuster Australia, in Canada by Ten Speed Press Canada, in New Zealand by Southern Publishers Group, in South Africa by Real Books, in Southeast Asia by Berkeley Books, and in the United Kingdom and Europe by Airlift Book Company.

Library of Congress Cataloging-in-Publication Data

Blocker Krantz, Lynn.
  To Honolulu in five days : cruising aboard Matson's S.S. *Lurline* /
Lynn Blocker Krantz, Nick Krantz, and Mary Thiele Fobian.
       p. cm.
Includes bibliographical references (p. 141).
  ISBN 1-58008-232-7
  1. *Lurline* (Ship)—History. 2. Ocean travel—History. 3.
Hawaii—Description and travel. I. Krantz, Nick. II. Fobian, Mary
Thiele. III. Title.
  G550 .B46 2002
  910.4'5—dc21   2001003113

Jacket and text design by Betsy Stromberg, based on a concept by Jeff Puda

First printing, 2001
Printed in China

1 2 3 4 5 — 05 04 03 02 01

For Pepper (Patricia Diane Thiele), who said,
"You guys should write something together,"
and for Eugene Savage,
who created the Matson murals.

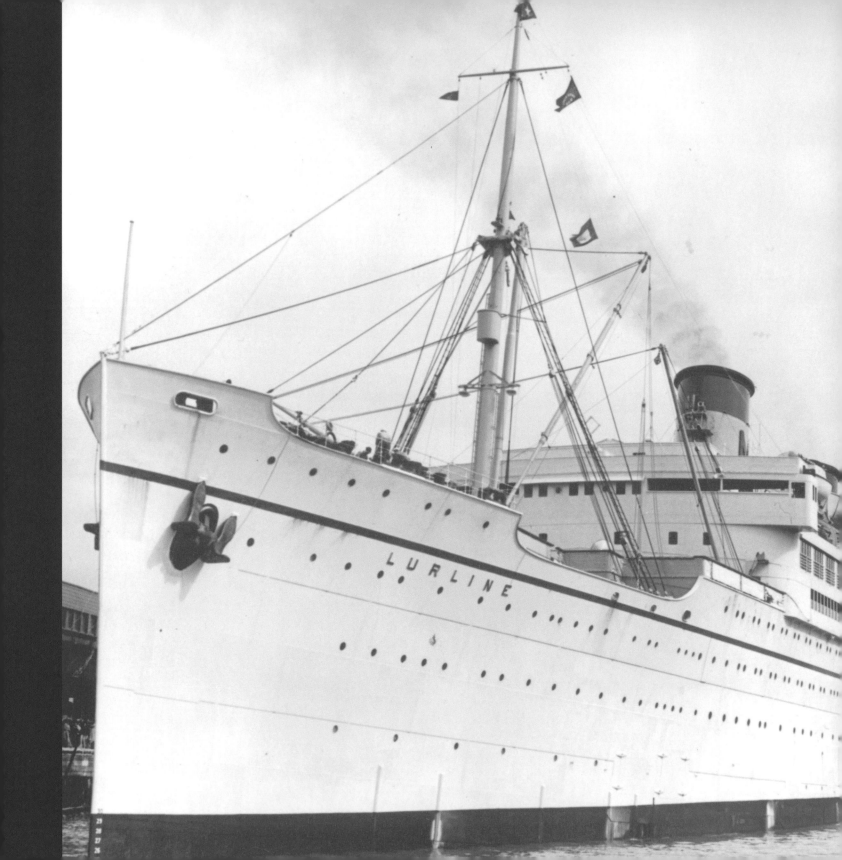

Contents

viii

FOREWORD

Since Matson Navigation Company was founded by Captain William Matson in 1882, there have been many milestones in the company's history, covering such diversified interests as oil exploration, military service during both world wars, the introduction of containerization in the Pacific in 1958, and even—briefly—the airline business. For most people, however, Matson's passenger liners and hotels arouse the fondest and most romantic associations.

Though Matson exited the cruise line business in 1970, the company continues to be strongly remembered for its famed "white ships" era that was instrumental in the development of tourism in Hawai'i. The enduring popularity of the artwork and related memorabilia produced for Matson's luxury liners and hotels is remarkable. Today, it is reproduced on a wide range of merchandise, including note cards, mousepads, calendars, and—thanks to Lynn Blocker Krantz, one of the authors of this book—a line of china, HawaiianaWare. For some, the art brings back memories of their travels aboard Matson's white ships or a stay at the Royal Hawaiian or Moana Hotels. For those too young to have experienced that era, the artwork is nevertheless equally appealing, as it represents classic Hawaiiana.

The ongoing attraction of Matson memorabilia directly reflects the careful attention to detail that distinguished "The Grand Manner of Matson." In addition to the white ships and Waikiki hotels, the experience was enhanced by celebrations such as Boat Day and keepsakes such as the menu covers created by Eugene Savage.

While Matson's complete history has been chronicled in a number of books, *To Honolulu in Five Days* is the first to focus exclusively on the celebrated passenger era. The book recounts the experience of traveling on one of the world's most famous passenger vessels, the S.S. *Lurline*. It features artwork created for brochures, menus,

S.S. *Monterey.*

THE SS MARIPOSA, 632 FEET LONG; 79 FEET BREADTH; GROSS TONNAGE 19,000; SPEED 22½ KNOTS

S.S. *Mariposa.*

and passenger lists, as well as actual recipes from Matson ships and hotels. Equally important, the account captures the essence of the time: fashion, social events, celebrities, music, and, of course, the journey itself.

Matson is very pleased that there is a now a book that accurately depicts this rich and colorful part of our history. We are confident that those who traveled on our passenger ships will find great pleasure in reliving their adventures; we are equally certain that many *malihinis* (newcomers) will enjoy the voyage in their imaginations.

Your adventure awaits. . . . *Aloha.*

Jeff Hull
Manager, Public Relations
MATSON NAVIGATION COMPANY

Eugene Savage: The Man Who Created the Matson Murals

Eugene Francis Savage.

Among the most treasured—and collected—memorabilia that passengers of Matson Navigation Company's S.S. *Lurline* have cherished over the years are the menu covers based on murals by Eugene Francis Savage. *Lurline* passengers could purchase the complete set of six menu covers, unfolded, for as little as two dollars. Today these souvenirs are in great demand by collectors, with a single menu cover in fine condition fetching prices up to two hundred dollars.

To create the menu covers, the mural images—eight feet wide by four feet high—were reproduced as nine-color lithographs, reduced to twenty-one inches wide by twelve inches high. In just the first four years of their use on the *Lurline*, Matson distributed over 250,000 covers to their lucky passengers.

Savage was born on March 29, 1883, in Covington, Indiana, to Hardy and Anna Weldon Savage. His father died three years later. Anna moved the family to Washington, D.C., where she raised her daughter and three sons in a classical musical environment and encouraged the boys to draw. Savage later remarked, "My brothers drew far better than I did, but they did not care for it as I did." He attended Gonzaga College High School and the Corcoran Gallery Art School in Washington, D.C.

Island Feast.

Upon his mother's death in 1900, fifteen-year-old Eugene joined his sister Mary in Chicago, where—even at that young age—he was able to obtain work as a commercial artist, and took night courses in fine arts at the Art Institute. By 1904, he was working only on weekends, spending his weekday mornings painting at the Art Institute and his afternoons painting at the Fine Arts Academy of Chicago.

Savage married Matilda Freitag, a physician, in 1908. Four years later, his painting *Morning* won the Prix de Rome, entitling him to three years at the American Academy in Rome, where he earned a bachelor's degree in fine arts in 1915. During his tenure in Rome, Savage wrote to his contemporaries at Chicago's Palette & Chisel Club, "Color is the medium as well as the object."

In 1923, Savage became an acting professor of painting at Yale, where he earned a second B.F.A. in 1924 and an M.A. in 1927. In 1928, he was appointed as the William Leffingwell professor of painting and design, a position he held throughout his tenure at Yale. President Herbert Hoover appointed Savage to the Commission of Fine Arts for painting in 1933, a position to which he was reappointed by President Franklin D. Roosevelt in 1937.

Upon receiving the commission to create six murals for Matson Navigation Company in 1938, Savage spent three months in Hawai'i making sketches and color notes, and researching the islands' history, botany, geology, and people. Deeply touched by the pageantry of the native culture, he chose this as the unifying theme for the Matson murals.

A God Appears.

Pomp and Circumstance.

Festival of the Sea.

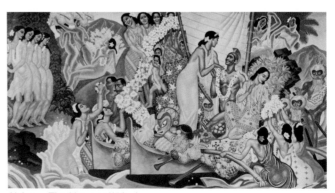

Aloha . . . The Universal Word.

By the time the murals were delivered to Matson's San Francisco office, war in the Pacific was imminent, so they went immediately into storage in the basement. And there they stayed until they made their debut on the S.S. *Lurline*'s menu covers when she returned to postwar cruise service on April 15, 1948. The menus—with lush illustrations of the islands' bounty on the outside, and a profusion of fare listed inside—truly celebrated abundance.

In 1951, Savage retired from Yale and became professor emeritus. He died in 1978 at age ninety-five, leaving a large body of work. His lone sculpture, the Mary Louise Bailey Memorial Fountain, stands in the Grand Army Plaza in Brooklyn, New York. His numerous easel paintings hang in museums and private collections. Savage's catalog of murals in public buildings throughout the United States is long and impressive; perhaps the most notable of these are *Armistice*, *Paths of Peace*, and twelve panels for the Rotunda (Elks Veterans Memorial, Chicago, Illinois); *The Spirit of the Land Grant College* (Humanities, Social Science, and Education Library, Purdue University, West Lafayette, Indiana); and *The Post as a Connecting Thread in Human Life* (Post Office Department Building, Washington, D.C.).

The Matson murals are considered the crowning achievement of Savage's career and were awarded the Certificate of Excellence, the highest possible award, at

Frank Burns at the linotype machine aboard ship. Each Matson passenger vessel had its own printshop. On a daily basis each shop printed 900 newspapers, 2,100 menus, and special cards for a variety of events.

the 1950 Printing of Commerce Exhibit of the American Institute of Graphic Arts. A complete set of the Savage menu cover images hangs in a permanent display in the Smithsonian Institute in Washington, D.C.

Four of Eugene Savage's Matson murals open the chapters of this book, accompanied by descriptions extracted from the original menu covers.

> My father loved Hawai'i—its landscapes, museums, and culture. He painted many Hawaiian easel paintings for himself following his trip there. Though he never returned to Hawai'i, he continued to paint Hawaiian scenes.
> —Dorothy Ann Crawford, daughter of Eugene Savage

Hawai'i's Decisive Hour

Matson Navigation Company and the S.S. *Lurline*

Matson Navigation Company's history is inextricably linked with the Hawaiian islands, but the story really begins in Sweden in 1849, with the birth of William Matson. His seafaring career began at age twelve, when he first shipped out as a "handy boy" on Swedish coastal ships. At age eighteen, Matson arrived in California and signed on with the schooner *William Frederick*, which carried coal to the Spreckels sugar refinery in San Francisco.

As a deck officer on the Spreckels sailing ship, Matson made several trips to Honolulu and saw an opportunity to transport sugar from the open port of Hilo to the mainland. Claus Spreckels helped Matson acquire the schooner *Emma Claudina*, which carried three hundred tons of food, plantation supplies, and general merchandise on its first voyage to Hawai'i in 1882.

Demand quickly outgrew the *Emma Claudina*'s capacity, and Matson swiftly put additional vessels into service. In 1901, Matson Navigation Company was incorporated, and its growth was rapid. When Captain Matson died in 1917, the company's fleet consisted of fourteen of the largest and most modern ships in the Pacific.

Following Captain Matson's death, Edward Tenney was elected president of Matson Navigation Company. Tenney had been serving as president of Castle & Cooke, a Honolulu firm that acted as agent for Matson in Hawai'i. The newly elected Tenney, along with Matson vice president William P. Roth, undertook an expansion of Matson operations that would capitalize on the increased interest in Hawai'i as a destination. More ships would be built to carry more passengers; hotels would be built and purchased. Matson Navigation Company saw the potential and responded, launching a romantic and legendary era of tourism in Hawai'i and the Pacific.

Captain William Matson.

Up the gangplank.

This colorful, whimsical description of the luxury liners' routes in the Pacific appeared in "Matson Lines to Hawai'i, New Zealand, Australia."

"LURLINE"

The luxury liner S.S. *Lurline* that carried so many happy travelers between the West Coast and Hawai'i from the 1930s into the 1960s was actually the third of five Matson Navigation Company vessels to bear that name; "Lurline" has been in continuous use by Matson Navigation Company since 1887.

In the early 1880s, Matson was asked to serve as skipper for a pleasure cruise on the Claus Spreckels family yacht, *Lurline*, and grew fond of the vessel's name. "Lurline" may be a variation of "Lorelei," the legendary mermaid whose siren song lured sailors to a watery death—a sea tale that was a particular favorite of the poetic Captain Matthew Turner, who built vessels for Spreckels and later for Matson.

THE FIRST *LURLINE*

The first *Lurline* owned by Captain Matson was a brigantine built by Turner for J. D. Spreckels and Brothers, who sold it to Matson in 1887. The 150-foot *Lurline* could carry a load of six hundred tons of sugar and accommodate a dozen passengers.

After being sold to Wallace Alexander in 1896, the brig *Lurline* went through several owners until 1915, when she became disabled off the coast of Mexico. She was sighted twice as a derelict at sea before going aground near the Straits of Magellan, a total loss.

The first *Lurline*'s arrival at Hilo (1887) was described in the *Honolulu Hawaiian Gazette:* "The new brigantine *Lurline* came gaily sailing into the bay on Friday, July 1, fourteen days from San Francisco, with flags flying, and Captain Matson and his bride aboard. She had all the appearance of a bridal yacht, as her hull was painted white, and her sails were fresh and new, and a considerable amount of bunting flying."

THE SECOND *LURLINE*

On January 11, 1908, the first steamer constructed for Matson Navigation Company was launched as Matson's second *Lurline* by the Captain's daughter, Lurline, from Newport News, Virginia. The *Lurline* arrived in San Francisco on May 20, 1908, and departed on her maiden voyage the following month, with a capacity for sixty-five crew and sixty-four passengers.

During World War I, the steamer *Lurline* was taken over by the U.S. Shipping Board and made nine trips to Honolulu and three to Manila. By 1928, when she was sold to Alaska Packers Association, she had completed 218 voyages. The rest of her career involved assignment to the Army Transport service during World War II and service to the Yugoslav Line (under the name *Radnik*) from 1947 until 1952. She was sold to shipbreakers in 1953.

The second *Lurline* was in Matson service for twenty years.

The third *Lurline* in 1932, prior to launching from Bethlehem Shipping Yard in Quincy, Massachusetts.

The second *Lurline*'s success and increasing demand for passenger service prompted Matson to build the 146-passenger ship, S.S. *Wilhelmina* (1910). In 1927, the company's deluxe passenger ship S.S. *Malolo* (Flying Fish) was put into San Francisco–Honolulu service and at twenty-two-knots was the fastest ship in the Pacific; her popularity led to the construction of the S.S. *Mariposa* and S.S. *Monterey*. Unflagging growth in commerce between the islands and the mainland continued to stimulate Americans' fascination with Hawai'i.

THE THIRD *LURLINE*

Designed by William Francis Gibbs and built at the Fore River Plant of the Bethlehem Shipyards in Quincy, Massachusetts, the S.S. *Lurline* was christened on July 12, 1932, by Lurline Matson Roth. (Contrary to popular misconception, the ships were not named after Captain Matson's daughter, for she wasn't born until three years after Matson acquired the company's first *Lurline*.) The steamship returned from her test voyage with a broom hoisted on her stacks, symbolizing a "clean sweep"—she had passed every item on her test run.

Matson Navigation Company's third *Lurline* was christened in 1932 by Captain Matson's daughter, Lurline Matson Roth.

THE NEW LINER ARRIVES

Sailing from New York City on her maiden voyage on January 12, 1933, the S.S. *Lurline* headed for San Francisco via the Panama Canal to round out the white fleet of sister ships—the S.S. *Malolo*, S.S. *Mariposa*, and S.S. *Monterey*—in providing luxury liner service to destinations in the Pacific. Her first voyage was a South Seas and Oriental cruise, and throughout her years of service she made runs to the South Pacific on special voyages: Christmas cruises to Acapulco in the years 1957 through 1961, and a South Pacific–Orient cruise in 1958 that lasted seventy-three days and called in such ports as Tahiti, Pago Pago, Auckland, Wellington, Sydney, Bali, Singapore, Bangkok, and Hong Kong. However, the *Lurline* is perhaps remembered most fondly for her five-day voyages between the West Coast and Hawai'i, plying a triangular route between San Francisco, Los Angeles, and Honolulu.

At the time the S.S. *Lurline* was put into service, the effects of the depression were still being felt throughout the U.S. Nevertheless, Matson's great white ships were steadily booked for travel to Hawai'i, as wealthy Americans vacationed in the islands in increasing numbers. This was due in part to Matson's extensive and innovative promotional campaign, with colorful brochures and advertisements enticing the would-be traveler:

> From the moment you sail, happiness plants its seeds within you. . . . It echoes in the music of a sea-going nightclub that strikes joy to the toes of those who love to dance. Tropical nights blend into carefree days in an utterly different pattern; starting with pleasure, ending with contentment.

The S.S. *Lurline* and her sister ships. From top to bottom: S.S. *Lurline*, S.S. *Monterey*, S.S. *Matsonia*, and S.S. *Mariposa*.

Fares and sailing schedules were printed in attractive brochures.

Natural color photograph, minimum fare First Class, outside stateroom S. S. Lurline

You'll always be glad
you made that perfect voyage to Hawaii

Details of *Matson Cruises to Hawaii and South Seas,* also *reservations at Royal Hawaiian and Moana Hotels* in Honolulu, from Travel Agents or MATSON LINE offices at New York, Chicago, San Francisco, Los Angeles, San Diego, Seattle, Portland.

S. S. LURLINE · S. S. MARIPOSA · S. S. MONTEREY · S. S. MATSONIA

Hawaii via Matson Line

Actual scene in the artistic Veranda Cafe aboard the S.S. LURLINE photographed en route Hawaii.

Following summer to Hawaii, in the luxury of the regal NEW Matson-Oceanic liners . . . equipped to anticipate the traveler's every desire. Establishing new standards in appointments, cuisine and service. Flawless living at sea, introducing flawless living ashore — in Hawaii. *Only a five day sail from California.*

Sailing every few days. LOW FARES will appeal.

☆

Only 10 days farther to New Zealand . . . 3 days more to Australia — fascinating lands of the Southern Cross. Samoa and Fiji along

the way. Low fares and all-inclusive-cost tours offer exceptional value. *Illustrated booklets, authoritative advice free at your Travel Agent's,* or MATSON LINE · OCEANIC LINE, New York, 535 Fifth Avenue · Chicago, 230 North Michigan Avenue · San Francisco, 215 Market Street · Los Angeles, 723 W. 7th Street · Seattle, 814 Second Avenue · Portland, Ore., 327 Southwest Pine Street.

S.S. LURLINE · S.S. MARIPOSA · S.S. MONTEREY · S.S. MALOLO

In the 1930s, "Boat Trains" established a schedule from New York and Chicago to San Francisco to coordinate with sailings of the *Malolo* and *Lurline*. Often there was so much demand that two train sections were needed to carry travelers to the city by the bay to board ship and continue on to the islands. The sleeping cars of the boat trains noted the ultimate destination, with names such as "Hawai'i," "Oahu," "Lanai," and "Honolulu."

Great Expectations

When the S.S. *Lurline* stopped through Los Angeles on her maiden voyage in 1933, an article in the *Los Angeles Times* expressed admiration for the ship's exquisite palette, cooling systems, broad decks, dozens of public rooms, two "plunges" (swimming pools), batteries of elevators, and geared turbines.

Certainly island-bound travelers had been given every reason to expect the very best from a voyage on the *Lurline*. An early brochure speaks of the ship's proud tradition: "It is implicit in every pillar and painting of the spacious interior. It speaks to you in every comfort and grace of modern sea-travel luxury. And it is indelibly recorded in your own contentment and approval, as one golden day follows another on your Matson voyage."

Focal points of ship life were the public rooms: lounges, dining rooms, dance pavilion, writing room, smoking room, and library. As a Matson publication expressed it, everything had been "designed, decorated, and appointed with brilliant originality."

Boat trains brought travelers to the West Coast to board Matson luxury liners and continue on to Honolulu.

White to Gray

When the bombing of Pearl Harbor changed the face of World War II, it also brought radical changes to the *Lurline*, her sister ships, and the entire Matson organization. The *Lurline* had left Honolulu on December 5, 1941, destined for San Francisco. At 10:15 A.M. ship's time on December 7, Commodore Charles A. Berndtson received news of the attack. The ship was diverted from her regular course at once (to avoid detection by enemy submarines that might be in the area) and began speeding homeward at twenty-two knots. The *Lurline*'s deck gang brought all available dark paint out of storage and painted the glass of every porthole and window so that no light from inside would reveal their location. Ironically, on that particular night a

A stateroom transformed to a bunk room for the *Lurline*'s service as a troop transport.

Throughout the war years, the flagship of Matson's white fleet wore a coat of gray.

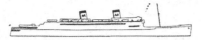

SOME INTERESTING FACTS ABOUT THE S. S. LURLINE

The S.S. LURLINE is 632 feet long with a beam of 79 feet and has a displacement of 26,000 tons. Speed in excess of 22 knots is provided by 25,000-horsepower geared steam turbines driving twin propellers 18 feet in diameter. Fuel consumption at a cruising speed of 19 knots is approximately 950 barrels of fuel oil per day. Fuel tanks hold 44,000 barrels of oil; enough to permit the LURLINE to cruise 21,000 nautical miles (24,000 statute miles) or to circumnavigate the globe without refueling. Our fresh water tanks contain a half million gallons of fresh water and our evaporators can make 80,000 additional gallons per day from sea water. Modern navigation aids include radar and loran.

The S. S. LURLINE is a self-contained "City Afloat" with accommodations for 722 passengers and operated by a crew of 425. Our "Seagoing City" has a hospital with a modern operating room, a library, laundry, beauty salon, tailor, store, print shop, barber shop, newspaper, telephone exchange, wireless office and recreational facilities. Food available per voyage to meet the demands of salt air whetted appetites consist of such qantities as 30,000 eggs, 20 tons of meat, three tons of fish, 15 tons of vegetables, two tons of butter, two tons of sugar, a ton of cheese and 1,600 gallons of milk.

The *Lurline,* a City Afloat.

full moon fully illuminated the great white ship from above. Traveling full speed ahead, the *Lurline* reached her home port in good time, docking in San Francisco at 3:27 A.M. on December 10.

As soon as the passengers disembarked, the *Lurline*'s conversion to a troop transport began. A 1946 Matson publication entitled *Ships in Gray* calls the transformation "an unavoidable devastation of luxury." The gleaming white exterior, the ship's name, and the Matson "M" on the stacks were quickly shrouded by coats of dull gray paint, and anti-aircraft guns were bolted to her decks. The changes that took place inside the ship would have shocked those who so recently had taken pleasure and comfort in the great lady's luxurious and commodious spaces. Everything was stripped—the mother-of-pearl inlay, rich paneling, plush rugs, and fine furnishings—to make way for tiers of bunks and spare, practical furnishings.

Originally designed for a capacity of 715 passengers plus crew and staff, as a troop transport the S.S. *Lurline* was revamped to accommodate up to 3,851 military personnel; however, the actual number aboard reached a maximum of 4,244 on December 20, 1942. At various times she carried not only troops, but also ammunition, bombs, other military supplies, battle casualties, Japanese prisoners, war brides, and children. Her routes ran between the mainland, Honolulu, Pago Pago, Australia, and every significant military base in the Pacific. In September 1943, she carried troops from San Francisco to Brisbane, Australia, and on to Bombay, India, where they would go on to become known as Merrill's Marauders. At the end of June 1945, she sailed for Marseille to redeploy troops to the Pacific. During her wartime service she logged thirty-one voyages totaling 388,847 miles, and carried 199,860 passengers for whom she provided over nine million meals.

The S.S. *Lurline* remained in war service under the United States Maritime Commission until May 29, 1946.

Luxury Travel Returns

It was amid much celebration and fanfare in San Francisco that the S.S. *Lurline* returned to passenger service on April 15, 1948, following a two-year, twenty-million-dollar refurbishment. After the bon voyage parties, the *Lurline* headed for the Golden Gate, saluted all along the waterfront by the traditional three whistle blasts wishing the great ship "good sailing." Richard M. Macfarlane, a reporter for the *San Francisco News* who was aboard the *Lurline* at sea, reported by radio telephone: "As of this day, real peacetime luxury travel is returned to Hawaiian service and all the romance and glamor of a cruise to the islands is embodied in this great white ship."

Five days later, the *Lurline* rounded Diamond Head, the majestic volcanic formation at the southeastern tip of Oahu. Awaiting her in the waters off Waikiki were more than two hundred small craft (including an eighty-vessel escort arranged by the Hawai'i Visitors Bureau) and, along the beach and at Aloha Tower, more than 150,000 people. This was a greeting imbued with an especially profound spirit of "*Aloha.*" The *Lurline* was bedecked with an eighty-foot orange *lei*, and the Territory of Hawai'i's Governor Steinback proclaimed this "*Lurline* Day."

Her service from the West Coast to Honolulu reestablished, Matson's S.S. *Lurline* continued to carry travelers to and from their vacations in paradise for another quarter of a century.

In 1963, the *Lurline* sustained turbine damage and was sold to Chandris Lines. Renamed *Ellinis*, she remained in service until 1980, when she was laid up at Piraeus, Greece. In 1987, fifty-five years after her christening, the noble ship was scrapped.

Captain Frank Johnson assisted Mrs. Lurline Matson Roth as she rechristened the S.S. *Lurline* for her return to luxury service following the war.

Colorful advertising invited travelers to experience the newly refurbished *Lurline*.

Masters of the Luxury Liner *Lurline* ★

1933–1946
Captain Charles A. Berndtson (became Commodore of the Matson Fleet in 1937)

1946–1953
Captain Frank Johnson

1953–1961
Captain Harold Gillespie (became Commodore of the Matson Fleet in 1955)

1961–1963
Captain Charles C. Wright (became Commodore of the Matson Fleet in 1975)

1963
Captain Hans O. Matthieson (became Commodore of the Matson Fleet in 1967)

Captain Charles A. Berndtson.

Captain Frank Johnson.

Captain Harold Gillespie.

Captain Charles C. Wright.

Captain Hans O. Matthieson.

THE FOURTH *LURLINE*

Following the sale to Chandris Lines, the great Matson steamship was gone but not forgotten. The name "Lurline" had become synonymous with luxury liner travel to the Hawaiian islands, and the public wanted their *Lurline*. Matson Navigation Company responded by rechristening their S.S. *Matsonia* (formerly the S.S. *Monterey*) as S.S. *Lurline* on December 6, 1963. The master of the fourth S.S. *Lurline* was Captain Hans O. Matthieson.

This vessel kept the *Lurline* legend alive for another seven years. In 1970, she was sold to Chandris Lines and renamed *Britanis*; she remained in service until 1996, when she was retired and dry-docked at Tampa, Florida. Sold to AG Belofin Investments on January 24, 1998, she was renamed *Belofin-1*. On October 21, 2000, this *Lurline* sank fifty miles west of Cape Town, South Africa, while en route to India for scrapping.

THE FIFTH *LURLINE*

In 1973, Matson once again bestowed the cherished name of *Lurline* when they launched a ro-ro (roll on/roll off) freight vessel, which continues to transport goods between the West Coast and the islands.

No longer does the luxury liner *Lurline* steam across Pacific waters; gone are the days when her departure from San Francisco set the stage for bon voyage revelry; and never again will she be greeted by a profusion of *leis*, *alohas*, and music in Honolulu Harbor. But the grand lady of the Pacific is still with us—in our photo albums and our scrapbooks, in the memories of everyone who spent five days out and five days back, and in your imagination as you share their experiences in the pages that follow.

Matson's fifth vessel to bear the name *Lurline* is this ro-ro freight ship, put into service in 1973.

The ship that began as the S.S. *Matsonia* and later became the S.S. *Monterey* was rechristened as the fourth *Lurline* in 1963.

Bon Voyage

*A*mong ancient Hawaiians, all events of importance called for a feast: births, marriages, weanings, even tax
gathering—every high point in their lives was signaled by a *luau*. The tradition of the island feast is brought to life in this mural that depicts preparations for a *luau*: An *imu* (pit) is readied to roast a pig, the heat from the scorching lava rocks carrying a trail of smoke toward the sky. A young man diligently pounds taro root to make *poi*. Island beauties hoist a basket of fruit above their heads while others enter-
tain guests with a traditional *hula*. Amid all the preparations and excitement sits the chief, awaiting the feast.

Island Feast by Eugene Savage.

SAILING DAY

They say that getting there is half the fun. It's a sentiment that might not be shared by today's airline travelers, but it certainly rings true in the memories of those who sailed aboard Matson Navigation Company's S.S. *Lurline* during the heyday of luxury liner travel to Honolulu.

From the moment travelers set foot on the gangplank, the festivities were underway. Boarding passengers often were accompanied by friends and family who came aboard to join the fun and wish them a good trip—or, in travelers' parlance, "Bon voyage!" In fact, the party was open to the public:

> What are you doing today? Why not take in a sailing of a Matson liner? . . . All ships are open to the public on sailing days—and you don't need to know anyone to join in on the fun.
>
> —*Guest Informant*

Boarding in San Francisco began at about one o'clock in the afternoon, with sailing at four o'clock. This was the beginning of a triangular route that normally ran outbound from San Francisco to Honolulu, then homebound from Honolulu to Los Angeles and back to San Francisco.

Matson Navigation Company's four luxury liners at San Francisco's Embarcadero, where Honolulu-bound passengers boarded the S.S. *Lurline*.

Margaret Enas, ready to sail in 1960.

Howard K. Morris with his *ukulele* aboard the S.S. *Lurline* serenaded passengers boarding at San Francisco.

Martin Denny family boarding the S.S. *Lurline*.

In these few hours—still at the dock—the *Lurline*'s steward staff made an exceptional first impression; throughout the voyage these individuals continuously proved that they were masters of the art of service: summon them, and nearly any need or desire was attended to promptly and graciously. Among their first duties on each voyage was the delivery of bon voyage baskets, floral arrangements, and well-wishers' notes. Also awaiting guests in their rooms were dining assignment cards. These specified the dining room and table where passengers would eat break-fast, lunch, and dinner, and indicated the first or second seating for dinner. Generally the elderly and families traveling with children were assigned the first seating, with couples and singles dining at the second.

Many travelers who hosted private bon voyage parties did so in their own rooms. However, larger parties—or those being thrown by VIPs—often were held in the ship's public areas, usually the ballroom. Occasionally passengers brought aboard catered provisions, or friends may have

Bon voyage greetings awaited passengers in their rooms.

Bon voyage baskets awaited passengers in their staterooms.

brought or sent ahead beautiful bon voyage baskets filled with fruit, cheese, and wine. Most often, though, food and drink for these celebrations were supplied by the ship. Matson's bon voyage menu offered champagne and other spirits, nonalcoholic punch, and such canapés as pigs in a blanket, stuffed eggs, several kinds of paté, cheeses, fresh fruits, and chocolates. On a typical sailing day, five hundred bottles of champagne and fifty pounds of caviar were consumed.

As enticing as these offerings were, passengers' guests had to leave the ship in a timely manner. One-half hour before sailing, the *Lurline*'s whistle (actually a loud horn) sounded one long blast, warning everyone that departure time was approaching. Fifteen minutes later,

two long blasts alerted travelers' guests that they must debark. When all were ashore who were going ashore, stewards distributed serpentine (streamers) among the passengers, who crowded along the railings and threw the streamers down to their loved ones on the dock. Then three long blasts of the whistle signaled that the anchor was being pulled up, and the hawser lines were tossed off the dock. No ifs, ands, or buts, the S.S. *Lurline* departed on time.

Slowly and carefully the *Lurline* moved away from the pier. Many well-wishers ran alongside to the end of the dock for a last farewell. Once out in the bay, the *Lurline* turned, passed beneath the Golden Gate Bridge, and on out into the Pacific, paradise her destination.

Three blasts of the ship's whistle indicated the *Lurline*'s imminent departure.

SFG 39   Golden Gate Bridge, San Francisco, California

Passing under the Golden Gate Bridge, the
Lurline entered the Pacific.

TICKETS, TRUNKS, AND TAGS

Sailing Day was the culmination of much preparation on
the part of travelers. A sea voyage to the Hawaiian islands
was by no means a spur-of-the-moment sort of trip. Tickets were purchased, often quite far in advance of the sailing date, from one of the sales offices in major cities such
as New York, Chicago, Los Angeles, Seattle, and Portland.
(Matson's home sales office at Powell and Geary Streets in
San Francisco was christened with the traditional bottle of
champagne by actress Dorothy Lamour in 1958.)

Bon voyage celebration.

"Hollywood's Dorothy Lamour needed six hearty swings before
she finally smashed open a 'thick skinned' champagne bottle
against the mock bow of a ship at the official opening on
December 2 of Matson's sparkling new Union Square ticket
office in San Francisco (at Powell and Geary Streets)."
—*Matsonews*, November–December, 1958

Tickets to Honolulu could be purchased at offices across the country.

Hawaii

S. S. LURLINE
S. S. MARIPOSA
S. S. MONTEREY
S. S. MALOLO

Nowhere but in the South Seas can such an array of diversions be compressed into a single summer vacation. Playing, resting, romancing on a Matson-Oceanic ship of sport- and- splendor. Wringing the last drop of pleasure from sun-flooded, sea-crisp days and moon-silvered nights on an opal ocean. Then more days and nights, as active or as lazy as you please, in play-and-languor-loving Hawaii. Only five days from California to its eternal May-time loveliness, forever cooled by fragrant trade breezes. At a low cost that urges "set sail".

SOUTH SEAS · NEW ZEALAND
AUSTRALIA · via Hawaii, Samoa, Fiji

About the storied lands of the Southern Cross the "Mariposa" and "Monterey" weave a charmed course. Commanding their superb luxury to speed you to New Zealand in 15 days, 3 days more to Australia. Topping the measure with all-expense (ship and shore) tours at startlingly low fares.

Learn the possibilities of a South Seas vacation. Obtain free illustrated booklet—at any travel agency, or

Matson Line · Oceanic Line
New York: 535 Fifth Avenue · Chicago: 230 North Michigan Ave. · San Francisco: 215 Market St. Los Angeles: 730 South Broadway · Seattle: 814 Second Ave. · Portland: 527 S.W. Pine St.

'ROUND THE WORLD VIA AUSTRALIA. NEW ROUTE! NEW SHIPS! LOW RATES! VARIED ITINERARIES!

For branch offices see Travelog on pages 10 and 11

Matson advertisement, June 1934.

Ticket and ticket folder.

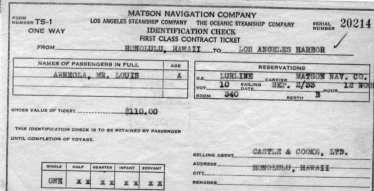

Accompanying the tickets was an early Matson pamphlet that offered suggestions on "What to Wear":

> Clothing of linen, white drill, pongees, or "Palm Beach" are popular all seasons with visitors to Hawai'i and the South Seas. Ordinary light-weight clothing of the mainland will be found entirely satisfactory for visitors to Hawai'i. Warm wraps should be taken for use in the higher altitudes. . . . A raincoat will be found useful.

In later years, prospective travelers received a charming leaflet entitled "Clothes for Your *Lurline* and Island Vacation," listing wardrobe suggestions. *Wahines* (women) were advised that a single evening dress and one cocktail dress would get them through the ocean voyage, but were cautioned, "Hats and gloves are seldom worn in Hawai'i." A white dinner jacket was suggested for *kanes* (men), with slacks and *aloha* shirts suggested for their stay in the islands. *Keikis* (children) would spend most of their time in bathing suits on the beach once they got to Honolulu, but for the *Lurline* trip an overcoat and sweaters were encouraged, as the first day out was usually chilly.

The leaflet also described long-standing fashions of the islands, providing ideas about what

Matson pamphlets gave advice about what to pack for a trip to the islands.

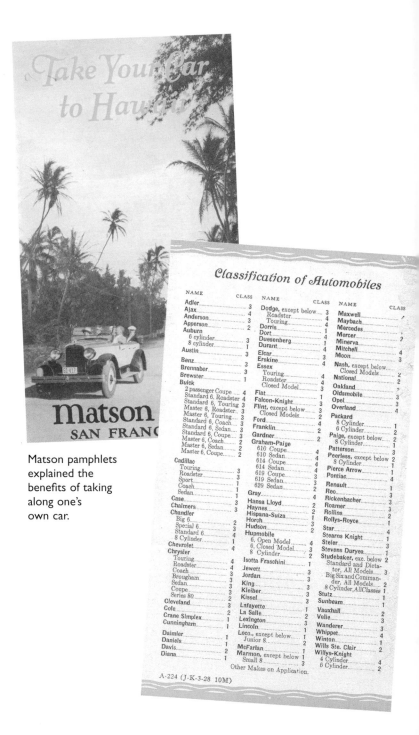

Matson pamphlets explained the benefits of taking along one's own car.

MATSON NAVIGATION COMPANY
215 MARKET STREET
SAN FRANCISCO · CALIFORNIA

HAWAII · SAMOA · FIJI · NEW ZEALAND · AUSTRALIA

June 10, 1941
PG 41156

Miss G. Burns
c/o Leslie Salt Company
310 Sansome Street
San Francisco, California

Dear Miss Burns:

In accordance with your call at our office, we are
pleased to confirm that we are reserving Bed B in
Cabin 503 at the $100.00 rate for Mrs. John Chulick
in the SS LURLINE sailing from San Francisco on
September 4th.

We are also reserving space for a Plymouth Coupe
in the same steamer and wish to advise that it will
be necessary to have the machine delivered at the
dock (Pier 32) not later than 5:00 PM on September
3rd.

We acknowledge a $10 deposit and have issued our
Receipt No. 94626. Final payment of $90.00 will be
due on this booking on August 1st.

Kindly request Mrs. Chulick to properly complete and

AUTOMOBILE CHECK & EXCEPTION REPORT
MATSON NAVIGATION COMPANY
THE OCEANIC STEAMSHIP COMPANY

Arrangements for transporting an automobile
required a little extra paperwork.

might be purchased upon arrival, and praising the bright colors and varied prints of the local fashions in bathing suits, sarongs, *muumuus*, and *holokus*.

Shopping at one's destination apparently was considered a very good idea by many travelers. In *Roger and I Go to Hawaii*, author Phyllis Warren shares the advice of a friend: "You can buy anything in Honolulu that you need, so don't tire yourself out shopping. Get your bathing suit there, and if you haven't an evening wrap...they have ravishing ones in the shops."

However, a great many clothes were likely to be packed, for the voyage to and from the islands alone constituted about ten days; in addition, travelers might stay in the islands from one to four weeks or more. This puts into perspective the 350-pound luggage allowance Matson granted each passenger (an allowance that remained in effect throughout the ship's lifetime).

In the days before rental cars, the affluent traveled not only with numerous steamer trunks, but also with their servants and personal automobiles.

As a passenger on *Lurline's* Honolulu-bound voyage during Christmas season 1934, Amelia Earhart brought along some interesting cargo. Tied down to the aft tennis deck was her Lockheed Vega. Two weeks later, on January 11, 1935, Earhart flew her aircraft from Wheeler Field to Oakland, California, the first person ever to fly solo from Hawai'i to California.

OFFER OF COMPLIMENTARY SERVICE
BY THE HONOLULU AUTOMOBILE CLUB
TO PASSENGERS BRINGING THEIR AUTOMOBILES TO HONOLULU

A representative of the Honolulu Automobile Club will meet this ship at quarantine in Honolulu Harbor and will be at the Purser's office until the steamer docks. The representative will, without cost to you,

1. Register your car, which will entitle you to drive your car for ninety days if you are a visitor, or for thirty days if you are to live permanently in Hawaii.

2. Service your car, which consists of checking tires, checking battery, and reconnecting battery terminals. (The law requires battery terminals be disconnected and gasoline drained at the time of loading.)

Before driving your car, however, you must appear in person at the Police Traffic Department, Bethel and Merchant Streets—approximately three blocks from the pier at which you dock—and present your driver's license. You will then be issued driver's license for Hawaii.

Gasoline to the same amount as was withdrawn at time of loading is refilled by the Matson Line.

MATSON NAVIGATION COMPANY.

Colorful luggage tags specified where bags should be delivered.

Having transported their baggage as far as the pier, travelers' worries on this score were over. Each bag was tagged to identify the Matson hotel (Moana, Royal Hawaiian, Princess Kaiulani, or Surfrider) where its owners would register when they arrived in Honolulu, then whisked away by stewards or bellmen for delivery directly to the appropriate stateroom. In this way, everything was handled swiftly and efficiently, both coming and going. Passengers' luggage awaited them when they arrived for their first glimpse of the cabins they would call "home" throughout the voyage.

BAGGAGE

Storing your excess luggage in the Baggage Room, on "F" deck, is almost like having it with you—without its being in the way. At convenient hours, which you may learn from the Purser's office, an attendant is in charge of the room to facilitate access to your baggage. In case of missing baggage, consult Room Steward, and notify Purser's office immediately.

Baggage information from a Matson pamphlet.

CABINS

Over the *Lurline*'s lifetime, Matson brochures depicted her wide selection of staterooms through both word and picture. Comfortable and attractive accommodations were provided for travelers on a budget as well as those who could afford to be more extravagant. Staterooms—even the most modest—provided a measure of luxury and ample space for two or three persons. With the wall and pullman beds folded into their recesses, they were transformed into sitting rooms furnished with easy chairs, dressing tables, wardrobes, and a screened-off vanity area.

The *Lurline*'s deluxe suites were more spacious than staterooms, and offered more in the way of luxurious furnishings and appointments.

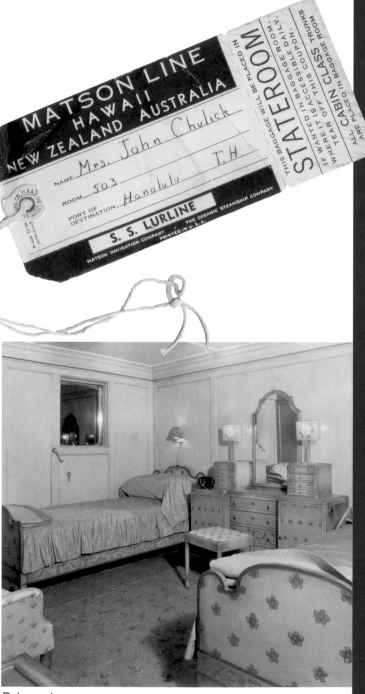

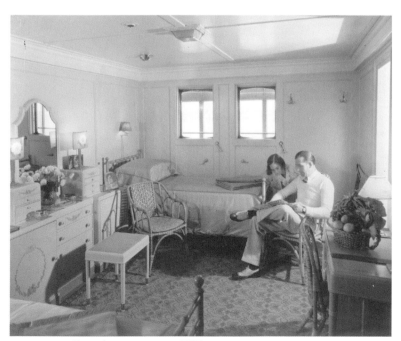

First class stateroom, 1930s.

Deluxe suite.

Lanai (porch) suites were the ultimate accommodations. Besides a sleeping area with vanity, there was a separate *lanai* sitting room with floor-to-ceiling picture windows opening onto a panorama of the Pacific. In addition, the *lanai* suites offered a dressing room with adjoining private bathroom.

Some staterooms had private baths, while others shared bathrooms. In either case, they were well outfitted and surprisingly roomy.

PROMPTINGS FROM THE FO'C'S'LE

"When in Rome, do as the Romans." When at sea, talk the language of the sea. Season your vocabulary with the salty flavor of the fo'c's'le. It's lots of fun, and besides it's practical. Of course, you know you go "above" and "below," not "upstairs" and "down." But there's more to it, and to assist you, here is a helpful list, properly crusted with brine:

Aft {abaft}	toward the stern
Amidship	the middle, or "waist," of a ship
Astern	in the direction of the stern
Bow	front of a ship
Bulkhead	partition
Chart	a sea map
Fathom	six feet
Fo'castle	seamen's quarters
Forward	toward the bow
Galley	kitchen
Gangway	passageway to a ship
Halyards	ropes for hoisting sails or flags
Heave-to	to slow down or stop a ship by bringing her bow to the wind
Hold	interior of a ship—space used for cargo
Knot	speed per hour in nautical miles
Latitude	distance directly north or south of the Equator
Lee-side	the side away from the wind (leeward)
Log	mechanical device for registering the distance run by a steamer

20

A primer on shipboard language from Matson's "The Ship is Yours."

Lanai suite, after the war.

Smoking room.

PUBLIC ROOMS

What *Lurline*'s passengers encountered in such rooms as the lounges, the dining salons, and the dance pavilion was a world of superlatives: the richest woods, the plushest rugs, and the finest furnishings.

The lounges served as the ship's social centers. This is where people came to talk, to have a drink, or simply to meet before continuing on to some activity elsewhere on the ship. The prewar décor of the *Lurline*'s main lounge incorporated gold and kapa shell. The cabin class lounge was more simply appointed, with an emphasis on comfort and charm.

Elegant bar room aboard the *Lurline*.

Main lounge.

Dining salon.

Like all areas of the *Lurline* frequented by passengers, the dining salons were redecorated several times over the life of the ship. In the early years, paintings of tropical birds and ships at sea adorned the main dining room.

The ballroom's open atmosphere called for a garden theme carried out by trellised walls, palm-filled nooks, and the informality of wicker and rattan furniture.

For those so inclined, the *Lurline* afforded special places for quiet contemplation, writing, and reading. The library was described as "a supremely satisfying room. In perfect harmony are the natural wood-paneled walls, the rare marine prints, the luxurious leather chairs, and the rich blue of the carpet. The books are chosen for their contents, as you will quickly discover, to make reading hours *really* enjoyable." The writing room sounds equally appealing: "When exciting events stir an urge to record them, the

WAIKIKI DINING ROOM

S.S. LURLINE

Guest _M/M HEBRANK_

Table No. _G6_

BREAKFAST   LUNCHEON   DINNER
8:15 a.m. to 10:00 a.m.   1:00 p.m.   7:30 p.m.

Your Host: C. C. Wright, Jr., Staff Captain

Dining table assignment card.

Dance pavilion.

writing room is an inviting retreat. Dainty desks and comfortable chairs, and paintings with narrative content encircling the walls. . . encourage one to write many a note, in a setting thoughtfully planned for that precise purpose."

A good book and a deep easy chair in a quiet spot is many a person's idea of the pleasantest shipboard leisure. Its companion pastime is spent over letters and diaries, writing at-the-moment impressions of the voyage. The *Lurline* has just the right place for both.

—Matson brochure

Library.

Writing room.

P.S. The enclosed was in L.A. paper. It should be good as it is a product of the Bell Laboratories, which Dr. Chapman thinks very top in science.

MATSON LINE
SAN FRANCISCO
LOS ANGELES
HAWAII

At Sea
Sept. 21, 1937

Ruth found these coupons in her stuff & that somebody might want them.

Dear Family:

This is Tuesday, just before dinner, and we are both up and feeling fit. I was sick and stayed in bed all day Sunday and until Monday noon. After that, food stayed down and I soon felt fine. Ruth made a lot of talk and resolutions about getting up Sunday but her efforts met with failure. She was dressed once and claimed she was going to breakfast but didn't make it. In the passageway was a fellow polishing a rail and from his hip pocket hung an extra towel. About that time Ruth was caught between nothing and nowhere so she quick

The writing room and library offered quiet space for writing to those back home and provided stationery and postcards.

Advertisements conveyed the experience of being waited on in Matson's Grand Manner.

S.S LURLINE HONOLULU

20th Century-Fox stars, Cornel Wilde and Patricia Knight (Mrs. Cornel Wilde) on the sun deck of the S. S. Lurline

PHOTO BY J N FREEMA

Thrill TO REMEMBER ALWAYS

Soon you can discover for yourself the lure that has drawn generations of passengers to Matson ships. It is more than the joy of sunny days on the serene Pacific, indolent or gay, as your mood desires. It is more than romantic nights beneath the glittering firmament of a world new to your eyes. It is everything combined to provide a vacation you'll remember always—superlative service which anticipates your every desire, good companionship, delicious food, swimming, dancing, playing, loafing, through glorious days made supremely comfortable — on ships as fine as you will find on any ocean.

Matson plans the finest in transportation by sea and by air

Matson

KNOWS THE PACIFIC

MATSON LINES TO HAWAII AND THE SOUTH PACIFIC
SAMOA • FIJI • NEW ZEALAND • AUSTRALIA
OFFICES: SAN FRANCISCO • LOS ANGELES • NEW YORK • CHICAGO

THE GRAND MANNER OF MATSON

Service aboard the *Lurline*—whether at a meal, or on deck, or directly to one's stateroom—was prompt, courteous, and gracious. Cuisine was fabulous and plentiful. These were just two elements of what is recalled as "The Grand Manner of Matson." In short, travelers dined like royalty, and were pampered and indulged twenty-four hours a day. The service of the stewards and the assistance of the pursers were evident; what was less obvious was all the organization and effort that went on behind the scenes. Matson historian Fred J. Stindt wrote:

> When a luxury liner backed away from the pier with its passengers in a festive and carefree mood, the ship became a "city" all its own. There were those who navigated the sea lanes, those who attended to the machinery for propulsion, and those who gave a variety of services which all added up to The Grand Manner of Matson.

A booklet described the concept at the heart of Matson's Grand Manner.

Thousands of pieces of letterhead and envelopes were just a fraction of the total stock of stationery—over three hundred kinds—used on each of the Matson luxury liners.

Behind the Scenes ★

Out at sea, the S.S. *Lurline* was essentially a city afloat, providing every necessity, convenience, and comfort imaginable. Preparedness was vital. So, while friends and family toasted passengers with wishes of "bon voyage," Matson employees were busily stowing unimaginable quantities of food for 725 passengers and 425 crew members.

Provisions necessary for a ten-day round-trip (that's 42,000 meals):

9,532 pounds of fresh fruit
1,921 pounds of frozen fruit
27,059 pounds of fresh vegetables
2,822 pounds of frozen vegetables
2,421 pounds of bread
85 pounds of yeast
858 pounds of bulk butter
1,040 pounds of butter pats
796 pounds of cheese
3,600 dozen eggs
15,575 pounds of milk and cream
382 gallons of ice cream
    and sherbet
4,736 pounds of fish (salted,
    smoked, and frozen)
5,360 pounds of game and poultry
1,132 pounds of lard, shortening,
    and margarine
15,976 pounds of meat
108 pounds of cooking wine
3,521 pounds of oils, pickles,
    sauces, and vinegars
109 pounds of spices and herbs
31 pounds of food colors and
    flavoring extracts

272 pounds of pasta
251 pounds of assorted nuts
5 pounds of paté de foie gras
88 pounds of special groceries
    for infants and others
2,494 pounds of miscellaneous
    groceries

Former auditor Louis Melson kept a meticulous accounting of the ship's expenditures, and by ten o'clock every night knew precisely the value of the food used to prepare that day's meals. The average cost of feeding one Matson passenger for one day in the pre-war days was $1.54.

Table Accoutrements ★

"*35,000 pieces of china and glassware on each Matson ship! 155,000 pieces always in reserve! 66,354 pieces of silverware on sea-going duty or in reserve on shore! No ship's 'set' of dishes or silverware is ever disrupted. It can be kept constantly intact by replacements from these reserves to fill up the ranks.*"

—Matson pamphlet
"The Building that Goes to Sea"

The *Lurline*'s staff and crew played a vital role in making the journey to Honolulu comfortable, luxurious, and memorable.

BELLBOYS

Your modern Aladdin's lamp—the telephone— will bring you a bellboy promptly at any time up to 10 p.m. It will, however, often expedite service if you tell the telephone operator what you desire. During the night, a steward is cheerfully at your service.

Many specialized food storage and preparation areas composed the *Lurline*'s galley.

WHO'S WHO ABOARD THE S.S. *LURLINE*

Before the ship sailed, the social director reviewed the passenger list and prepared an unofficial "Who's Who" list to be distributed to the staff and crew. As you might imagine, this was a list of those passengers who were to be given particularly special attention. It frequently included the names of political figures, royalty, sports figures, heads of corporations, and stars of the silver screen.

Among the many celebrities who traveled on the S.S. *Lurline* were the following:

Bette Davis.

Mickey Rooney.
Cheers!

Gracie Allen and
    George Burns
Jack Bailey
Mr. and Mrs. Jack Benny
Ann Blythe
William "Hopalong
    Cassidy" Boyd
George Brent
Lloyd Bridges
Hoagy Carmichael
Cyd Charisse
June Christy
Claudette Colbert
Linda Darnell
Bette Davis
Frances Dee
Irene Dunn
Jimmy Durante
Charlie Farrell
Alice Faye
Tennessee Ernie Ford
Clark Gable
Barbara Hale and
    Bill Williams
Jack Haley
Edith Head
Barbara Hutton
Mahalia Jackson
George Jessel
Spike Jones

Dr. John Harvey Kellogg
The King Sisters
Alan Ladd
Dorothy Lamour
Carol Lombard
Julie London
Myrna Loy
Marie MacDonald
Tony Martin
Joel McCrea
Jack Oakie
Helen O'Connell
Mary Pickford
William Powell
Amelia Earhart Putnam
Ronald and Nancy Reagan
Alvino Rey
Buddy Rogers
Mickey Rooney
Rosalind Russell
Mr. and Mrs. Tommy
    Sands
Jimmy Stewart
Gail Storm
Robert Taylor
Shirley Temple
Toni Twins (Marianne and
    Charlotte Guice)
Mr. and Mrs. Mel Torme
Margaret Whiting

It's likely that Miss Beverly Lake was on the Who's Who list for a 1948 voyage of the *Lurline*. A senior at UCLA in 1948, Beverly had won the title of "Dream Girl" in a contest connected to a popular movie, *Mr. Blanding Builds His Dream House* (starring Cary Grant and Myrna Loy). The first prize was a trip on the S.S. *Lurline* to Hawai'i and an all-expenses-paid two-week stay at the Royal Hawaiian Hotel.

Celebrity or not, everyone aboard the *Lurline* when she put out to sea was about to experience luxury, indulgence, fabulous cuisine, and entertainment en route to Honolulu.

"Dream Girl" Beverly Lake.

Mr. and Mrs. Jack Benny with a young traveler.

Captain Charles Wertz showed George Jessel around the S.S. *Lurline*.

Hoagy Carmichael and Linda Darnell.

Fun and Frolic at Sea

To the Hawaiians of old, fishing was not only a means of livelihood, but also an art and a sport. In the *hukilau* it became a gay, exciting community festival. Some of the fish were caught up by the canoes and carried in. The greater part were hauled to the beach and dumped out, flopping on the sand. The bigger the catch, the louder the shouts of triumph. Prayers of thanksgiving were offered up to the gods of the sea for their bounty, and the day became a holiday ending in a gala village festival.

Festival of the Sea by Eugene Savage.

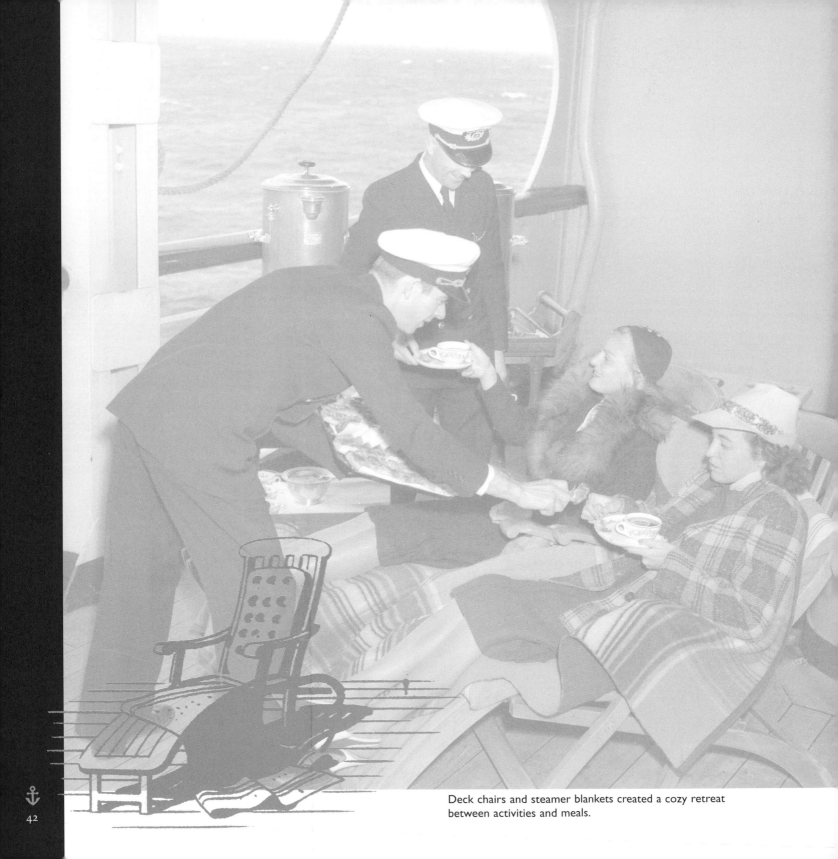

Deck chairs and steamer blankets created a cozy retreat between activities and meals.

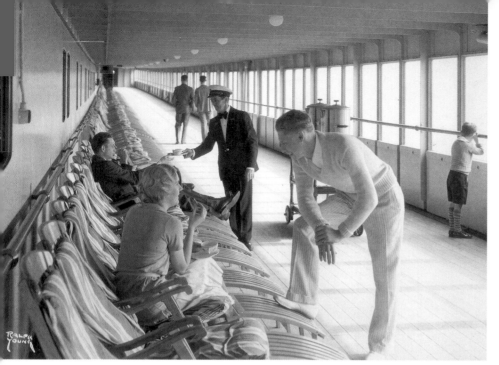

Deck chairs were the perfect place to rest, read, or converse.

ON DECK AND AROUND THE SHIP

By the first morning out, most passengers had acquired their "sea legs" and were ready for some fun in the sun. Day or night, a variety of amusements was available.

During the day, outdoor activities beckoned. Those attuned to the fine art of relaxing opted for a stroll around the promenade deck, or simply lounged. In the 1930s, steamer chairs and rugs were available "on application to the deck steward," at a rental fee of $1.50 each for the duration of the voyage.

The more athletically inclined took part in skeet shooting, deck tennis, shuffleboard, table tennis, and other games. The outdoor pool offered swimming and a gathering place for anyone wanting to get a head start on a terrific Hawaiian tan.

Matson instituted some "firsts" in terms of offering sports facilities on their liners in the Pacific. In 1962, the first golf driving platform was installed on *Lurline*'s main deck aft, so the golfers drove the balls off the stern and far out into the sea. A few months later, bowling alleys were introduced on the sports deck.

Tennis.

Skeet shooting.

Shuffleboard.

The swimming pool was also known as "the plunge."

At ten-thirty every morning, hot bouillon and tea were brought to passengers on deck; as the ship drew closer to the islands and air temperatures grew warmer, mid-morning's hot drinks were replaced by a refreshing scoop of sherbet. Luncheon was promptly at noon—sometimes served buffet-style on deck. Hearty entrees were nicely balanced by a light and refreshing fruit salad.

Mid-morning, bouillon and tea were served on deck.

Hawaiian Fruit Bowl ★

SERVES 6

This fruit salad was the sort of dish offered at the deckside buffet luncheon in the 1950s, when food trends reflected a fondness for sweet and minty liqueurs. Special meals often ended with a plain scoop of vanilla ice cream that had been "Frenchified" with a drizzle of crème de menthe. This fruit salad features the mint flavor right in the dressing.

1 pint plain yogurt
Juice of 6 fresh limes
1/2 cup of peppermint schnapps
1 cup fresh orange sections
1 cup fresh pineapple, diced into
    1/2-inch chunks
1 cup banana, sliced 1/4 inch thick
1 cup seedless grapes

1 cup fresh mangoes, diced into
    1/2-inch chunks
1 cup fresh papayas, diced into
    1/2-inch chunks
1 cup fresh strawberries, halved
1 cup miniature marshmallows
1/2 cup grated coconut
6 lettuce leaves
Fresh whole strawberries
Fresh mint sprigs

To prepare the dressing, combine the yogurt, lime juice, and schnapps in a small bowl and set aside.

Place the remaining ingredients in a large salad bowl. Add dressing and toss gently. Chill until ready to serve. Serve the salad on lettuce leaves, garnishing each serving with whole strawberries and mint sprigs.

Chief steward Jack Abramson and cookbook author Victor Bennett collaborated in preparing a Hawaiian fruit salad.

Those interested in bingo or a game of cards gathered somewhere comfortable and welcoming, such as the lounge or card room—or perhaps in the smoking room, where dominoes, chess, cribbage, and Scrabble were available from the stewards.

Like all other activities aboard the *Lurline,* bingo and card games drew a good crowd.

For many years, slot machines were available, but in 1952 they were outlawed by the federal government's Kefauver Crime Commission. When orders to get rid of the machines came down from Matson headquarters, the *Lurline* was in the general vicinity of the Farallon Islands near San Francisco. Here, at about three o'clock in the morning, the slots went over the railing. According to an eyewitness, a Catholic priest traveling on the *Lurline* made the best of the situation by administering mock last rites as the slots went into the watery depths, never again to spill forth a booty of coins.

A leisurely game of cards on deck.

WOODEN HORSES, REAL MONEY

Perhaps not quite *all* the comforts and pleasures of the mainland were available aboard ship, but when something couldn't be provided, arrangements were made for the next best thing. In the case of those longing for a day at the track, a substitute was offered to tide passengers over.

The veranda served as a ballroom in the evenings, but during the day its wooden dance floor was covered with a felt track for those who yearned to play the ponies. "Horse racing" involved six wooden horses and a curved track divided into several sections. Bets were placed by buying tickets on the horses, numbered 1 through 6. The dice were thrown by an officer or a volunteer from among the passengers; one die represented the horse, and the second die indicated how many spaces forward the horse was to

be moved. A member of the crew moved the appropriate horse forward on the track.

Margaret Enas traveled to Honolulu on the *Lurline* in 1960 and recalls the horse races:

> Having never been to the races here at home, I somehow managed to win—as a matter of fact, enough to more than cover the cost of my ticket, which was approximately $200.

Dorothy Lamour was aboard the *Lurline* in 1941, and impressed everyone with her friendliness and approachability. She graciously—and enthusiastically—served as cashier for the horse races as well as bingo games. A former

Scorecard for the wooden horse races.

Lurline purser, Earl Rollar, recalls Lamour fondly: "She was the greatest person you'd ever care to meet."

Speaking of cashiering, Judge Gordon Minder (a former *Lurline* purser) recalls: "It was Matson's policy in those years not to cash personal checks. One day a passenger asked to cash a check and I informed him of Matson's hard and fast rule. However, he persuaded me to bend the rule when he turned out to be Henry Morgenthau, Jr., the Secretary of the U.S. Treasury."

Some folks are gamblers and others aren't. But it's a sure bet that nearly everyone aboard wanted to know more about *hula* and other Hawaiian traditions.

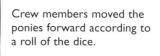

MATSON LINE
SAN FRANCISCO
LOS ANGELES
HAWAII

On the sea.

Dear Folks:
Well when ever I get comfortable Olive think I ought to write to some one. There are horse races on the deck right now. The horses and riders are wooden of course with numbers. Then two pretty girls, with gay colored jockey caps on, shake dice; a chap also clad in a loud cap reads off the numbers. Then the deck steward, who for some reason doesnt feel the need of the race attire, moves the horses over the hurdles etc as

Shipboard horse races were something to write home about.

Crew members moved the ponies forward according to a roll of the dice.

LET'S *HULA!* . . .
AND STRUM A FEW BARS

A fun-loving and enthusiastic tour guide who accompanied many groups on trips aboard the *Lurline* had made a good impression on Matson's management, and in 1952 they hired him as the *Lurline*'s first entertainment director. He went by the name of Howard K. Morris. (Never was an initial more packed with potential than this one, signifying the middle name of *Kekaiohuakalanikiekie*—which translates roughly to "Born on a rocky coast under adverse circumstances on a day of overhanging clouds when the surf was dashing on the rocks.")

The talented, versatile, and extremely likable Morris immediately established "The *Lurline* Institute of Hawaiian Music and Dance" (dubbed "the lightest-hearted educational institution afloat"), and proclaimed himself *Ka Kuma Hula O Ka Pakipiko* (the *Hula* Teacher of the Pacific).

It was Morris's belief that "anybody who can walk up the gangplank can dance the *hula*." En route to Honolulu, he taught passengers to *hula* to "The Hukilau Song"; those who completed the course were eligible to seek a postgraduate degree on the return voyage by mastering the moves of "Little Brown Gal." A *Saturday Evening Post* travel writer asserted that "Dignified businessmen and shy school teachers kick off their shoes and wiggle their hips aboard the *Lurline*."

Ukulele classes were not so strenuous as *hula*—nor as hilarious! By the end of the first lesson, everyone was strumming "*Wailana*" and had learned to properly pronounce "ook-oo-lay-lay"; the expression "yuke" was *kapu* (taboo).

During his tenure on the *Lurline*, Morris awarded thousands of *palapala* (graduation certificates) for *hula* dancing and *ukulele* playing.

Hula lessons.

Certificate for *hula* class graduates.

Howard K. Morris taught ukulele lessons aboard the *Lurline*.

MESSAGE IN A BOTTLE

Though no degrees were awarded, another high point in shipboard diversions was the "message-in-a-bottle activity." Passengers were provided with bottles, corks, and paper, and instructed to write a note that included their home address. A couple of dollars for postage, the note—and sometimes small memorabilia—were placed in the bottle, which was then corked, sealed with candle wax, and thrown overboard. In the 1960s, a passenger named Ross E. Perry tossed a message in a bottle off the *Lurline* just 387 miles out of Los Angeles; it was found washed up on the Maui coastline fifteen years later.

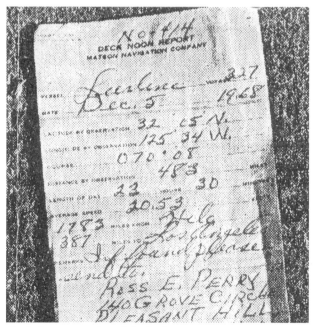

Bottled up memories of the *Lurline*.

KEIKI CORNER

Matson's passenger ships were well prepared to make the voyage memorable for children as well as adults. A playroom and a playground were provided, and a junior hostess entertained children who were traveling with their parents.

A typical day of children's shipboard activities began with the *Keiki* Town Meeting in the lounge, followed by a movie (for example, Disney's *Cinderella*). After joining their parents for lunch, the kiddies met in the marine veranda for the *Keiki* Talent Show rehearsal, a Fire and Lifeboat Drill on the promenade deck, and then back to the children's playroom for *Keiki Hula* Time. Late in the afternoon, while their parents were having cocktails, the children had their own *Keiki* Punch Party before joining the family for dinner. The children's program sometimes included exercise, a picnic lunch, a treasure hunt, and other fun. Occasionally a surprise visit added special excitement. One mother who traveled with her children remembers: "There always seemed to be a celebrity aboard. I recall in particular the time Mr. William Boyd—Hopalong Cassidy—was aboard. He was warm and friendly and was a special treat for all the youngsters."

In July 1935, the *keikis* aboard S.S. *Lurline* might have thought they were on the Good Ship Lollipop when America's sweetheart, Shirley Temple, joined them on a trip to Honolulu with her parents.

Shirley Temple on the *Lurline,* 1935.

Playgrounds for children were provided on all Matson's passenger ships.

THE CAPTAIN'S CHAMPAGNE PARTY

An extravagant champagne party preceded many superb dinners aboard the *Lurline*. It was a gala event, long remembered by anyone who experienced it. In the lounge, all the ship's officers lined up and greeted each and every passenger in attendance. Then, naturally, everyone's attention turned to that effervescent libation that brings a special mood, a sense of celebration, to any gathering: champagne.

> The French prefer Champagne chilled rather than iced, believing that extreme cold hurts the flavor. But the English and American palates find that the extreme cold assists the "pick me up" character of sparkling wine. A favorite continental method of chilling wine is to wrap the bottle in wet cloth and place it in a draught for a short time. In no circumstances is ice ever put into wine. It should be remembered that cold, as well as subordinating the alcoholic elements of the bouquet, diminishes the facilities of taste.
> —*Matson Service Bulletin,* February 23, 1934

Champagne glass bearing Matson's logo.

Commodore Harold Gillespie, master of the *Lurline* from 1953 until 1961, was known to take microphone in hand to welcome everyone to the champagne gathering. Later—as the cocktail party came to an end—he took it up again, observing, "*Champagne tonight, real pain tomorrow morning.*"

And the bubbly flowed freely. For those who liked the *idea* of champagne, yet wanted a stronger cocktail, "The Matson" was just the thing. Whatever they were drinking, everyone was urged to take up a song sheet and join voices.

The Captain's Champagne Party.

CAPTAIN'S CHAMPAGN PARTY—

Captain's Champagne Party

ON BOARD S. S. LURLINE
HONOLULU TO CALIFORNIA

COMMUNITY SINGING ON THE LURLINE

1—Enjoy Yourself
Enjoy yourself,
It's later than you think.
Enjoy yourself,
While you're still in the pink.
The years go by,
As quickly as a wink.
Enjoy yourself . . . Enjoy yourself,
It's later than you think.

2—I Wonder Who's Kissing Her Now
I wonder who's kissing her now,
Wonder who's teaching her how.
Wonder who's looking into her eyes,
Breathing sighs, telling lies.
I wonder who's buying her wine
For lips that I used to call mine.
Wonder if she ever tells him of me,
I wonder who's kissing her now.

3—Put Your Arms Around Me
Put your arms around me, honey
Hold me tight.
Huddle up and cuddle up
With all your might.
Oh Babe, won't you roll them eyes,
Eyes that I just idolize.
When they look at me . . . My heart
Begins to float,
Then it starts a-rocking like a motor boat.
Oh! Oh! I never knew any girl like you.

4—Ma
Ma, he's making eyes at me,
Ma, he's awful nice to me,
Ma, he's almost breaking my heart.
I'm beside him,
Mercy let his conscience guide him.
Ma, he wants to marry me.
Be my honey-bee,
Every moment he gets bolder,
Now he's leaning on my shoulder,
Ma, he's kissing me.

5—We Were Sailing Along
We were sailing along,
On Moonlight Bay.
We could hear the voices ringing,
They seemed to say.
You have stolen my heart,
Now don't go way.
As we sang "love's old sweet song"
On Moonlight Bay.

6—When I Grow to Old to Dream
When I grow too old to dream,
I'll have you to remember.
When I grow to old to dream,
Your love will live in my heart.
So kiss me, my sweet,
And let us part.
And when I grow too old to dream,
That kiss will live in my heart.

Champagne Party goers were given song sheets and encouraged to sing along.

The Matson Cocktail ★

This interesting cocktail recipe was created in the 1930s. The kümmel imparts an intriguing caraway flavor. (Note that a full shot glass contains 1.5 ounces.)

SERVES 1
⅓ shot kümmel
½ shot cognac
1 sugar cube
Chilled champagne
Piece of lemon peel
Chilled 6-ounce martini glass

Pour kümmel and cognac over crushed ice in a shaker and shake gently. (Do *not* add champagne to the shaker.) Place the sugar cube in the chilled martini glass. Strain kümmel and cognac into the glass. Add champagne to fill, and float lemon peel on top. Sip slowly—it's very unusual! (If you don't have a shaker, chill kümmel and cognac in advance and pour directly over a sugar cube in a chilled martini glass, then fill with champagne and garnish with lemon peel.)

Captain Johnson hosted the world-renowned *Aloha* Dinner.

THE CAPTAIN'S DINNER

Perhaps the most memorable shipboard occasions were the elegant evening meals. The large dining salon was always festively decorated, the tables adorned with graceful floral arrangements and laid with the finest linen, china, and silver. Stemware and flatware bore the distinguished Matson logo.

On each voyage, an especially elaborate dinner was held. In the early days this was called the *Aloha* Dinner, but it later came to be known as the Captain's Dinner. Regardless of the name, it occasioned extra touches such as gold

A menu for the elegant Captain's Dinner.

The Matson Flag ★

Captain Matson's second wife, Lillian, took a voyage to Honolulu on the *Roderick Dhu* in 1901. She felt that it was time for Matson Navigation Company to have its own flag, so she gathered some signal flags, cut them up, and stitched the pieces together to form a new Matson flag: seven stars encircling the letter "M."

and white decorations, strolling musicians, and photographers. The tables' centerpieces always included miniature Matson flags.

The diners were in a festive mood and had taken special care with their wardrobe for the evening. Men appeared in the dining salon wearing dinner jackets, escorting ladies dressed in glamorous gowns. The second seating often was a veritable fashion show as the ladies swept into the salon.

Passengers came into the dining room through the main entrance, and a steward directed them to their assigned tables. The captain's table was just a few steps

Lurline social directress Dolores Niles and chief purser William R. Sewell (seated second and third from the left) enjoyed many festive dinners with passengers.

to the left of the front door—not the stuff that grand entrances are made of. On one particular voyage, film star Rosalind Russell was among the guests invited to sit at the captain's table. Miss Russell waited each evening until nearly everyone else was seated, then entered through the dining salon's *back* doors, winding her way between tables through the entire length of the room, all eyes upon her.

Dining aboard the *Lurline* was a culinary delight, amazing vacationers from the mainland with the abundance and variety of foods. Chefs mingled classic French cuisine with more traditional mainland fare, as well as exotic island delicacies. Dinner menus typically featured eight or more entrées and as many as fifty or sixty individual items, some of them familiar and others unusual.

As the natural accompaniment to fine food, wines were selected and stocked with great care. An impressive Service Bulletin dated February 23, 1934, provided the steward staff with a great deal of information and advice. The bulletin's opening paragraphs set forth the philosophy upon which Matson wine service was based:

> Probably nothing in the world is so steeped in tradition as wine. Yet in spite of all the ritual with which the connoisseur surrounds it, the appeal of wine is essentially a simple one—the delight of the primary senses of sight and smell and taste.
>
> The return of wine and the rising tide of appreciation for better balanced, more harmonious living warrant a review and examination of the old customs. They represent a proud and glamorous era with which the spirit of contemporary life, with its eager interest in the refinements and delights of gracious dining, is finding itself in more and more accord.

Wine steward Arthur J. Speiser poured innumerable glasses of champagne throughout his career with Matson.

Ice cream server and tablecloth bearing the Matson "M" logo.

Matson's Wine Recommendations ★

Matson Navigation Company's 1934 Service Bulletin set forth guidelines for pairing wines with the delicious meals served in its shipboard dining rooms.

Hors d'oeuvres
Light dry wines, generally white. Light Sauternes, dry Catawba, Alsatian and Rhine wines, white Burgundies.

Oysters
Light dry wines, always white—Chablis, dry Champagne.

Melon
Medium wines. Medium Sherry, Madeira, sweet Sauternes.

Soup
Light dry wines, generally white. Sherry, Graves, Beaujolais (Pouilly), other white Burgundies (Montrachet, Volnay, Meursault).

Fish
Light dry wines, always white. Hock, Moselle, Alsatian wines, dry Champagne, white Burgundies.

Entrée (light meat, chicken, etc.)
Light red or white wines. Beaujolais, light Clarets.

Meat
Medium wines, generally red. Claret, Burgundy, Chianti.

Poultry
Medium wines, red or white. Medium Champagne, Hock, Clarets, Burgundies.

Game
Medium wines, generally red. Claret, Burgundy.

Salad
No wine.

Cheese
Medium wines, generally red. Claret, Burgundy, Port.

Dessert
Heavy, sweet wines. Port, heavy Sauternes, Madeira, sweet Champagne.

Coffee
Brandy, liqueurs.

Last but not least, the Service Bulletin revealed "The Important Vintage Years." Thank goodness Matson served Côte d'Or Burgundies only from 1917, 1919, 1921, 1923, 1926, 1928, and 1929, and rejected those from the "bad years" of 1913, 1927, and 1930!

I love everything that's old: old friends, old times, old manners, old wine.

—Oliver Goldsmith, quoted on a *Lurline* dinner menu dated May 1, 1941

DANCING AND ROMANCING

After dinner, the *Lurline*'s elegantly garbed passengers convened in an expansive space that was known variously over the years as the ballroom, the pavilion, and the veranda. No matter the name, the inviting surroundings and the strains of the ship's orchestra made the dance floor irresistible. How many steps trod across that smooth, gleaming wood, and in what configurations! Waltz, rumba, cha-cha, fox trot—then jitterbug, jive, and swing—and, when the 1960s rolled around, the twist, jerk, and watusi.

> Come sunset you fall into the festive mood of evening on Matson's Pacific. After cocktails and a superb dinner, your ship becomes a glittering world of glamorous nightlife with festive parties, dancing, and excitement. There's a late, late club open 'til all hours around the piano bar, too. (No matahari could command more royal amusements.)
>
> —*Matson brochure*

Away from the stress of everyday life and the constraints of society, who could resist the hypnotic effects of moonlit skies and soft trade winds? In this romantic environment, it's not surprising that young people often fell—or thought they had fallen—madly in love.

Though the silver screen has made much of shipboard nuptials, marriage ceremonies were not performed on the *Lurline* unless the bride and groom brought their own minister. Perhaps no weddings took place aboard ship, but honeymoons certainly did. Clark Gable and Lady Sylvia Ashley—who married on December 20, 1949—celebrated their first Christmas together just days later aboard the S.S. *Lurline*.

From the 1930s through the 1960s, passengers dressed to the nines and flaunted their fancy footwork across the ballroom floor.

Newlyweds Clark Gable and Lady Sylvia Ashley honeymooned aboard the S.S. *Lurline*.

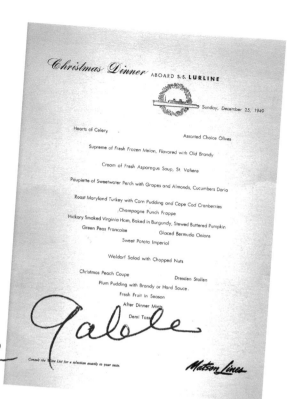

Christmas Dinner ABOARD S.S. LURLINE

Sunday, December 25, 1949

Hearts of Celery   Assorted Choice Olives

Supreme of Fresh Frozen Melon, Flavored with Old Brandy

Cream of Fresh Asparagus Soup, St. Valiere

Paupiette of Sweetwater Perch with Grapes and Almonds, Cucumbers Doria

Roast Maryland Turkey with Corn Pudding and Cape Cod Cranberries
Champagne Punch Frappe
Hickory Smoked Virginia Ham, Baked in Burgundy, Stewed Buttered Pumpkin
Green Peas Francaise   Glaced Bermuda Onions
Sweet Potato Imperial

Waldorf Salad with Chopped Nuts

Christmas Peach Coupe   Dresden Stollen
Plum Pudding with Brandy or Hard Sauce
Fresh Fruit in Season
After Dinner Mints
Demi Tasse

Consult the Wine List for a selection exactly to your taste.

Matson Lines

It wasn't only passengers who found floating to Hawai'i on the *Lurline* irresistibly romantic. Acquaintances and friendships among the staff and crew sometimes blossomed into lasting relationships. A well-known couple who worked together on the *Lurline* and later married were social directress Dolores Niles and chief steward Jack Abramson. Another romance between *Lurline* staffers began in 1958, when C. J. "Jim" Faber sailed on the *Lurline* as auditor and Marian Laughlin signed on as a nurse; they met on a Sailing Day in January and were married the following September.

The ocean adventure inspired romance, and the brisk sea air and an evening of dancing conspired to whet the appetite. No matter the hour, the S.S. *Lurline* was ready to take care of its passengers' cravings in grand manner.

Chef Techtman inspected the *Lurline*'s Christmas buffet lunch.

Hawaii

The latest celebrity to linger at Waikiki. Expectant stay-at-homes this Christmas will mourn the defection of their dear Kris

... the beloved old humbug slipped off on a Matson-Oceanic liner bound for Hawaii, and his deserted votaries will have to be contented with the untried charity of a proxy.

Not even a saint should be expected everlastingly to keep on the job of bulldogging a string of reindeer and shinning down sooty chimneys.

Personally, we'd barter any time a couple of weeks of snow and sleet for a South Sea voyage to a cozy corner of sun-warmed Waikiki. *Sir to you, Santa.*

Possibly a twinge of conscience may prompt Santa to canter over to the chimney of an old volcano and fill up the beach sandals. But with that concession to ritual, he will forget his plush and ermine upholstery (nice but very stuffy) don a bathing suit, swim in velvet waters, doze on golden sands and listen to Yuletide greetings in the lispings of the surf.

Age-old native melodies will be his evening carols, a bemused stroll under the silken caress of an amber moon, the final touch of beauty to an amazingly new, *utterly different* Christmas— in Hawaii. . . . . *Aren't you interested?**

*The giant "Lurline", "Mariposa", "Monter___" or "Malolo" sail every f___

Captain Robert McKenzie and his wife, Joan.

Marian Laughlin and Jim Faber met while working on the *Lurline* and later married.

MIDNIGHT SNACK

Matson's designation of the late-night feast as a "snack" is one of the great understatements of all time. Some folks say that eating roast beef and turkey drumsticks and other rich foods before bedtime will bring on nightmares, but you can be sure that this modestly named buffet made many snackers' gustatory dreams come true.

> In the late evening there is nothing more intriguing than a foray on the chef's midnight snack.
> —*Matson brochure*

At home, a midnight snack might be a dish of ice cream or a piece of toast. On the S.S. *Lurline*, it was an outrageous expanse of food, laid out in absolute glory. Tables were spread with the whitest damask, lavishly decorated, then heaped with tiers of delectable dishes.

Gleaming platters proffered roasted meats—turkey, ham, and beef—glazed with *chaux froid* and extravagantly garnished. These shared the spotlight with smoked fish, mousses, and terrines. Betwixt and between these hearty offerings, a profusion of salads and side dishes filled every cranny of available space.

Such culinary indulgence was a memorable part of the voyage for the *Lurline*'s passengers. Former purser Earl Rollar recalls, "It was just like eating in a big New York nightclub every night." It's hard to imagine that it could get tiresome, but Rollar confesses that the staff and crew sometimes couldn't wait to get to port so they could go get a simple hamburger.

After dancing the night away and "a little something" to tide one over until morning, there was neither time nor energy for anything more than one last stroll around the deck, sleepy eyes gazing at the moon's reflection on the sea beneath a canopy of stars.

Passengers returning to their quiet and luxurious staterooms found that even the last moments before sleep were touched with the Grand Manner of Matson: the sheets had been turned down and a plate of fresh fruit placed on the bedside table. It was time now for *moeʻuhane* . . . a Hawaiian dream.

The chef's extravagant Midnight Snack.

Evening on the Lurline: You enter an enchanted world ruled by a moon you've never seen

Night on the Pacific is like no night you've ever known, and the moon it holds weaves a rare enchantment.

Here's all the peace and beauty you could ever want. Here's the escape you've waited for, the world apart where every mood can find expression and no care can ever reach.

Here on the Lurline, loveliest ship afloat, you'll rediscover yourself . . . live a new and vibrant life of your own choosing—restful or gay, exciting or quiet.

Plan your vacation cruise to Hawaii on the new Lurline. Your travel agent will be glad to help you.

Matson
TO HAWAII

Here's music, too...for dancing or listening. Movies are shown, and there is other entertainment if you desire it.

You meet new friends...interesting shipmates for your life on the Lurline, people you'll always enjoy knowing.

You learn the magic of the gentle Pacific, and the moments you spend in its spell will be part of your life forever . . . something special you'll never forget.

Hawai'i

The word is *Aloha,* idiom of an ancient, warmhearted people. It signifies friendship— "affection, esteem, love." As a salutation it expresses welcome; at parting it means farewell . . . not with finality, but implying the hope that "we shall meet again." In this scene of an island queen greeting a neighboring chief and his consort, Eugene Savage dramatizes the meaning of *aloha* in one gesture. . . the presentation of its age-old symbol, the flower *lei.* In Hawaiian culture, the thought is expressed in many ways: in dancing and entertainment, in feasts, in gifts of food. In the language of old Hawai'i, *"Aloha"* said in welcome implies boundless hospitality.

Aloha . . . The Universal Word by Eugene Savage.

BOAT DAY

Even before the *Lurline* was in sight of Oahu, the soft, balmy air of the islands came to greet her, carrying fragrances unique to Hawai'i. As she rounded Diamond Head, those on deck caught their first glimpse of Waikiki and came under the spell of swaying palms and rolling surf.

At just that moment, the ship's breakfast bell sounded, forcing a choice between food for the body or a feast for the eyes. Warmed by the tropical sun and caressed by the trade winds, passengers gathered at the railings to take in the breathtaking panorama before them. A Matson brochure described the experience:

> And then . . . Hawai'i! On deck to greet the brilliant dawn, as cool trade winds sweep away the mists of lingering night. . . . The first view of the jagged cliffs of Oahu brings a wave of excitement, an ineffable feeling of romance and mystery. It is a sudden realization that all the tales of Stevenson and Melville were true, must have been true. Those passionate childhood instincts for adventure flare into being once more, and despite your modern liner, you feel as if you were pacing the quarter-deck of a four-masted schooner.

Now that the *Lurline* had come to the island, the island seemed to come to her. Small craft carried friends, family, and welcoming officials who climbed aboard, greeting the *malihinis*—"newcomers"— with a hearty "*aloha*" and draping *leis* around their necks. A press boat brought reporters eager to get the scoop on traveling celebrities. Outrigger canoes scattered a welcoming festoon of fresh-flower *leis* on the water. Tugs came alongside, carrying hundreds of greeters, their arms full of *leis* for the arriving passengers. Young men dove for coins tossed over the ship's railing, in a ritual described in Sydney Clark's *Hawaii*:

The Hawaiian diving boys are gathering in swarms, ready to show their heels to the sky when passengers toss coins into the water. Coppers they will scorn as being invisible. Even nickels and dimes are viewed with mild contempt, though not ignored. But a quarter will produce a wondrous underwater scramble, and one of the faces will presently emerge with the bulky coin stowed in its cheek. These are never invisible and never lost, nor is any young mouth ever too crowded to take in one more such coveted coin.

Back in the 1930s, the importance and regularity of Matson steamship arrivals in Honolulu were signified by the expression of time in terms of "*Lurlines*" or "*Matsonias.*" It was quite common to hear locals say, "She is staying for two *Lurlines,*" or, "He will leave *Lurline* after next."

Boat Day originated in the early 1870s, when it was the custom for the Royal Hawaiian Band to play whenever King William Lunalilo left the island on his many voyages.

By the 1880s, when Matson ships began arriving in Honolulu, the tradition had changed from a farewell to a greeting, extended enthusiastically by well-wishers crowded on the Matson pier. In the early days the celebration was called "Steamer Day" rather than "Boat Day," but the sentiment was the same: "*Aloha. . . .* Welcome to Hawai'i!"

The tug *Mikioi* welcomed the elegant S.S. *Lurline* to Honolulu.

Hula dancers greeted new arrivals.

Coin divers.

The S.S. *Lurline* arrived in Honolulu amid a flurry of serpentine.

VIS
ALLOW
SHIP
PRIOR

Brimming with as much anticipation as those aboard ship, Honolulu's businesspeople and shopkeepers took a brief hiatus to participate in the welcoming festivities, filling the docks as hundreds came to greet the great white ship. As the *Lurline* dropped anchor, serpentine crossed the space between ship and pier, propelled by cheers and shouted greetings. *Hula* dancers, fragrant *leis*, and haunting island melodies mingled to imprint upon the newcomers a sense of magic that would forever color their memories.

The Royal Hawaiian Band welcomed arriving passenger ships.

Royal Hawaiian bandleader Henri Berger.

During this era, the Royal Hawaiian Band was under the direction of Henri Berger, a German musician appointed by King David Kalakaua in 1883. On Boat Days, the band always played "Hawai'i Ponoi"—first the national anthem of the Kingdom of Hawai'i, later the territorial anthem, and ultimately Hawai'i's state song. It was composed by King David Kalakaua and set to music by Berger.

For many years, "Song of the Islands" was sung at Boat Days by one of Hawai'i's most beloved soloists, Lena Machado (known as "Hawai'i's Songbird"); she also captivated the *malihinis* with "*Aloha Oe*," written by Queen Lili'uokalani, Hawai'i's last monarch.

A Lofty *Aloha*

As the *Lurline* approached Honolulu Harbor, a tower on Oahu's shore came into view. It rose high above everything else at the waterfront as if it wanted to be the first to bestow an "*Aloha.*" It was, indeed, the Aloha Tower, embodying Honolulu's welcoming spirit.

Aloha Tower.

Honolulu's city fathers conceived of the Aloha Tower as a symbolic greeting for the shiploads of visitors arriving regularly in Honolulu Harbor in the early part of the last century. Erected alongside Piers 10 and 11, the Aloha Tower was completed in 1926, when it was the tallest building on the island, at 184 feet, 2 inches, and topped by a forty-foot ship's mast that serves as a flagstaff. On each of the building's four sides are a clock face, a balcony, and the word *"Aloha."*

Down the gangplank the visitors came, to set foot finally on Oahu, where their carefree island days had now truly begun. Their luggage was once again whisked away, only to arrive later—by apparent magic and no effort on their own part—at the hotel they had chosen for their stay in Honolulu, and placed in the correct room before they even registered.

Many Matson travelers were gifted with *leis* while still on the ship. Their senses were assailed by the colors and fragrance of plumeria, wild ginger, and tuberose, and the textures of leaves, vines, berries, and even shells. At first, mainlanders may have thought it extraordinarily indulgent to swathe oneself in flowers, but the *lei* sellers at the pier really were irresistible, and you only live once, so a second *lei* often was the traveler's first island purchase. When they learned the price (a mere quarter in 1939), it suddenly seemed reasonable to wear not one, but two—perhaps three, maybe four.

In the islands, the custom of giving *leis* in friendship is an ancient tradition. Like the word *aloha*, the *lei* signifies a range of meanings: hello and goodbye, the joy of welcome and the grief of farewell.

Shirley Temple and Duke Kahanamoku.

Gracie Allen and George Burns.

Albert Finney received leis and kisses.

Even the *Lurline*'s captain received a festive *"Aloha."* Captain Frank Johnson welcomed by Hilo Hattie.

Baggage was transferred to and from the hotels by the Honolulu Construction and Draying Co., Ltd.

Amelia Earhart Putnam and Judge Ben Lindsay were fellow passengers on the *Lurline* in 1934.

> If you have not known the thrill of a Hawaiian flower *lei*, you have never lived.
> —Matson's *Aloha* Magazine

Laden with *leis* and clutching their *Matson Travel Guides* in hand, the *malihinis* hailed a taxi and instructed the cabby: "Waikiki."

Hawaii via Matson Line

ALOHA NUI!

The original of this Ilima Lei was worn only by the royal family during the days of the Hawaiian monarchy. The Ilima flower is the official flower of the Island of Oahu.

Matson Lines

HAWAIIAN GUIDE

Facts You Should Know about Hawaii

Issued by the Matson Line

HAWAII'S *Musical Language* ★

Visitors are immediately impressed by the mellow, musical sound of Hawaiian words. Though not essential, it adds greatly to enjoyment to acquire a small vocabulary and an ear for correct pronunciation.

Reduced to English characters, there is an alphabet of only 12 letters: the five vowels, A, E, I, O, U, and seven consonants, H, K, L, M, N, P, and W. Vowels are sounded (with minor variations) generally as in Latin languages, consonants as in English, except that in a few words W is pronounced like V. Thus the name of the Territory—Hawaii—becomes Hah-wye-ee, or occasionally is heard Hah-vye-ee. Some of the more common Hawaiian words are:

Ae—Yes
Akamai—Clever
Alanui—Street, road
Aloha—Friendly salutation, love
Aole—No
Ewa—Roughly, northwest
Hale—House
Halekula—Schoolhouse
Halepule—Church
Halekuai—Store
Hana—To work
Haole—White man, foreigner
Heiau—Old native temple
Hele mai—Come here
Hele Wawae—Walk
Hiamoe—Sleep
Hokele—Hotel
Holoku—Mother hubbard
Huhu—Angry
Hukilau—Fishing festival
Ilio—Dog
Ipo—Sweetheart
Kaa—Car
Kaa ahi—Railroad train
Kahuna—Priest, doctor, teacher
Kai—Sea
Kamaaina—Oldtimer
Kamailio—Talk
Kanaka—Man
Kapu—Prohibited
Keiki—Child
Keikikane—Boy
Kaikamahine—Girl
Ko—Sugar
Kokua—To assist, help

Kope—Coffee
Kuai—Buy, sell
Kulikuli—Be still
La—Sun
Lanai—Porch, veranda
Lei—Wreath
Like-pu—The same
Lio—Horse
Luau—Feast
Maanei—Here
Mahalo—Thanks
Mahope—Bye and bye
Maikai—Good
Makai—Toward the sea
Make—Dead
Malaila—There
Mamua—Before, in front of
Mauka—Toward mountains
Mele—Music
Mokuahi—Steamer
Nui—Large
Palaoa—Bread
Pali—Cliff
Pau—Finished, done
Pehea oe—How are you?
Pilikia—Trouble, bother
Pipi—Cow, beef
Poi—A native food
Popoki—Cat
Wahine—Woman
Wai—Water
Waikiki—(Used commonly in Honolulu), in the direction of Waikiki
Wikiwiki—Hurry

HAWAIIAN MOTTO—*Ua mau ke ea o ka aina i ka pono*— "The life of the land is preserved in righteousness".

Fragrant, colorful *leis* could be purchased from vendors immediately upon disembarking the ship.

Matson provided passengers with a complimentary travel guide that included a list of Hawaiian words that might come in handy during their island visit.

A HONOLULU LEI VENDER

THE GRAND HOTELS OF WAIKIKI

Long ago, nature created the enchanted place that has come to be known as Waikiki. Generations of Hawaiian royalty reveled in this paradise, playing ancient games and sports, and enjoying *luaus* and *hula*.

To this pristine beach Matson Navigation Company brought the tradition of its Grand Manner, beginning with the company's initial venture into hotel operations in the late 1920s and continuing until 1959. Over those decades, Matson's goal was "to offer luxury both afloat and ashore."

Matson's entry into the hotel business was the brainchild of Edward Tenney and William P. Roth. Tenney was president of both Matson Navigation Company and the Honolulu firm of Castle & Cooke, and Roth was vice president and general manager of Matson. Their first step in developing hotel accommodations on Waikiki was construction of the Royal Hawaiian Hotel, followed quickly by its acquisition of the Moana Hotel. Matson eventually built the Surfrider and the Princess Kaiulani to complete its quartet of Waikiki hotels.

A brochure cover offered a view of the Royal Hawaiian and the Moana–Seaside Hotels from the sea.

ROYAL HAWAIIAN *and* **MOANA - SEASIDE HOTELS**
ON THE BEACH AT WAIKIKI, HONOLULU, HAWAII

The Royal Hawaiian Hotel

The Seaside Hotel cottages, about 1924. These cottages were located where the Royal Hawaiian Hotel now stands.

In 1925, Matson Navigation Company, along with Castle & Cooke and the Territorial Hotel Company, obtained a fifty-year lease from the Bishop Estate on more than fifteen acres of Waikiki shorefront. This beach area, formerly called "Helumoa," had been a retreat for King Kamehameha I, and its grove of ten thousand coconut palms had at one time been the site of Queen Ka'ahumanu's summer palace. In the earliest days of the twentieth century, the Waikiki Seaside Hotel was located at the site of the present Royal Hawaiian.

The hotel was designed by the New York architectural firm of Warren & Wetmore, and built by the Honolulu contracting firm of Ralph E. Woolley. Groundbreaking took place on July 6, 1925, and construction was completed sixteen months later, at a cost of nearly five million dollars.

Dubbed "the Pink Palace," the now-famous coral-pink stucco building combined the cupolas of California Mission style with an overall Spanish-Moorish theme that appealed to the American public of the 1920s, who had been enchanted by the Rudolph Valentino movies so popular at that time.

The porte cochere.

Vacation Opportunities AT THE *Royal Hawaiian* HOTEL

ON THE BEACH AT WAIKIKI

Royal Hawaiian Hotel
HONOLULU
Ready to receive guests on FEBRUARY 1, 1927

Honolulu's finest hostelry, the Royal Hawaiian, at Waikiki, under the same management as the famous Moana and Seaside hotels, which it adjoins, will open on February 1, 1927.

The Royal Hawaiian contains 400 rooms, all with private bath and shower. The hotel also has many delightful suites with an open air private lanai (veranda or porch) overlooking a marvelous view of Waikiki beach or the colorful mountains. All rooms are outside. The minimum rate will be $12 a day, each person, American plan only.

The Royal Hawaiian, Moana and Seaside guests will have the use of a new private 18-hole golf course ready this January.

Our offices in New York, Chicago, Seattle, Los Angeles and San Francisco will quote you rates and make bookings.

TERRITORIAL HOTEL COMPANY, LTD., *Honolulu, T. H.*
Matson Navigation Company, San Francisco, *Mainland Representatives*

NEW YORK: 30 East Forty-second Street;   LOS ANGELES: 510 West Sixth Street
CHICAGO: 140 South Dearborn Street   SEATTLE: 814 Second Avenue

BULLETIN No. 73   *San Francisco, October 20, 1926*

Opening Night

On the evening of February 1, 1927, the Royal Hawaiian staged its grand opening—a black tie affair for twelve hundred guests, including Princess Abigail Kawananakoa (who might have been crowned queen had the monarchy survived) and Territorial Governor Wallace R. Farrington.

On the long-awaited night, dinner (at the pricey rate of ten dollars per plate) began at 7:30 P.M. and continued for two hours. Following the meal was a pageant, directed by Princess Kawananakoa, which reenacted King Kamehameha's landing on Oahu.

The dining room.

These dresses, worn at the Royal's grand opening in 1927, are on display in the lobby.

These women distributed *leis* to opening night guests.

The pageant ("colorful and semi-barbaric," said the press) depicted the arrival of King Kamehameha the Great on Oahu and included a fleet of fifteen canoes carrying fierce warriors, oarsmen, and *kahili*-bearers. As the king stepped ashore, he was greeted by five beautiful princesses, each representing a major Hawaiian island. Kamehameha then sat upon a throne to enjoy a program of dances and chants.

—*David Eyre in
"The Night They Opened the Royal"*

The Royal Hawaiian Band was present for this great occasion, conducted by Captain Henri Berger. During the meal, fourteen members of the Honolulu Symphony played chamber music.

A pageant depicted the arrival of King Kamehameha the Great on Oahu.

In the Grand Ballroom, twelve hundred people danced to the music of the Royal Hawaiian Band. Overhead, opulent chandeliers hung from a ceiling embellished with highly decorated beams.

Behind the Scenes ★

"Your new hotel, The Royal Hawaiian, is without doubt the finest resort hotel I have met up with anywhere in the world, and richly deserves the widest patronage, not only because of the charm of its location and its magnificent appointments as to the creature comforts, but because of its able management."

—Correspondence from John Oliver LaGource, Associate Editor, *National Geographic* magazine, printed in *Aloha* magazine, May 1927

The Royal Hawaiian's first manager, Arthur Benaglia, drew together an impressive staff dedicated to serving the needs and desires of the hotel's guests. Upon opening, the Royal Hawaiian's staff list included:

95 waiters
40 room boys
20 bellboys
10 elevator operators
5 phone operators
2 doormen
2 pages
8 lobby boys
60 kitchen staff (the ice cream maker alone had three assistants!)

The hotel also was well equipped, with the following service supplies on hand in anticipation of the opening.

38,624 dishes
28,284 glasses
20,292 knives, forks, and spoons
22,573 towels
30,988 sheets, blankets, and bedspreads

In its first five years, the Royal Hawaiian Hotel served over fourteen thousand guests. Room rates in the mid-1930s were eleven to seventeen dollars for a double room, and this was on the American plan—with all meals included!

Royal Hawaiian dining room staff.

The first baggage handlers were dressed in typical Oriental garb.

A Royal Welcome

On Boat Days—those exciting occasions when a Matson passenger ship had arrived—the Royal held a welcome party. The newly arrived guests were in a festive mood, the music was wonderful, and the setting, after all, was Waikiki. Dancing took place outside on the Ocean Lawn.

Upon arrival in Honolulu, the *Lurline*'s crew stayed aboard ship, but members of the purser's department were permitted to stay (at no charge for the rooms) at the Royal Hawaiian. For many of them, these welcome parties are among their fondest recollections of the great old hotel.

Under the stars at the Royal Hawaiian.

Dancing at the Royal Hawaiian.

When Dorothy Lamour traveled to Hawai'i on the *Lurline* in 1941, naturally every man on the ship and on the island assumed that the beautiful actress already had an escort for the welcome party. But that was not the case, so—not one to miss a party—Miss Lamour asked her room steward from the *Lurline* to accompany her that evening. The happy fellow's good fortune created quite a stir among his peers as he arrived at the festivities with Dorothy Lamour on his arm.

Guest Rooms

The four hundred guest rooms were lavishly appointed, all with private baths. Forty rooms featured *lanais* overlooking the grounds and the beach. Furnishings were of bamboo, rattan, and wicker, and bamboo awnings protected all out-side windows. The fine damask linens were produced by James D. Hardy Company of New York. No detail was overlooked; every need was anticipated, down to a pin-cushion provided in every room.

Ocean view from guest room.

Guest room with *lanai*.

A special edition of the *Honolulu Star-Bulletin*, printed in conjunction with the Royal's grand opening, described the accommodations:

> Sea green walls and deeper green rugs—sugges-tive of leaves . . . drapes and lampshades in soft apricot . . . and the pictures are quaint old-fashioned flowers in gay shades. . . . The beds have jade green and coral bedspreads . . . the pincushions are jade green, covered with lace and honeydew silk ribbon to match the lampshades.

Royal Hawaiian ballroom.

ROYAL-HAWAIIAN-HOTEL
WAIKIKI BEACH
No.24 Date FEB-1-1927
Warren and Wetmore
- Architects -

Public Areas

Public rooms such as the Persian Room and the Byzantine Ballroom were decorated with rich rugs and fabrics of ornate designs, gleaming wood furniture, and tropical plants everywhere. Light from tall arched windows reflected off the highly polished wood floors.

> If you're going to be very grand, go to the Royal Hawaiian Hotel. It's quite the last word.
> —*Highlights on Honolulu*

The Persian Room (now called the Monarch Room) was an open-air salon overlooking the beach. Diners there selected from such delicacies as *paupiette* of *mahimahi* Kauilani and a starstruck dessert by the name of *coupe* Lillian Russell. Of the many glamorous dishes served at the Royal, one that has persisted as a favorite over the years is the Royal Hawaiian bread pudding.

During the day, the glamorous and fashionable gathered in the hotel's broad *lanais* and shaded courts, some of them clustering around brightly decked tables for tea, bridge, or a midday meal. Afternoon tea was served on the Coconut Grove *lanai* at 3:30 P.M. every day, with *hula* and songs provided by the Royal Hawaiian Girls Glee Club. Luncheon could be taken here, or out on the beach promenade, where fine food was accompanied by the sights and sounds of Waikiki Beach.

Royal Hawaiian lounge.

Luncheon on the beach promenade.

Royal Hawaiian Bread Pudding ★

"A bit of sweet makes the meal complete."
—*from a Royal Hawaiian dinner menu, August 1, 1929*

The Royal Hawaiian Bread Pudding (served with Crème Anglaise) is the hotel's signature dessert. This recipe comes directly from the Royal Hawaiian's kitchen.

SERVES 8 TO 10
Preheat oven to 400°.

Fill a tea kettle with water and heat. (This hot water will be used when you place the pudding in the oven.)

15 eggs
1 cup granulated sugar
6 cups milk
1 pint heavy cream (do not whip)
6 tablespoons pure vanilla extract
1 long loaf French bread, sliced
3/4 cup golden raisins

Combine eggs and sugar in a large mixing bowl and mix at low speed for three minutes.

Add milk, cream, and vanilla to the egg-sugar mixture, continuing to mix for four minutes. Strain and set aside.

Arrange bread slices in a buttered 9 by 13-inch baking pan. Sprinkle raisins more or less evenly over the top of the bread. Pour enough of the egg mixture over the bread to fill the pan about one-quarter full. Allow it to soak into the bread for about five minutes. Push down the surface of the bread occasionally with a spoon to speed up the absorption of the egg mixture. Then add the rest of the liquid and allow to stand for ten minutes.

Meanwhile, butter one side of a piece of foil large enough to cover the baking pan. Cover the pan with the foil (buttered side down). Place the pan inside a larger baking or roasting pan. Place both pans in the preheated oven, then quickly pour enough of the hot water into the space between the two pans to bring the water level about three-quarters of the way up the sides of the inside pan. Bake the pudding for 1 1/2 hours.

Crème Anglaise ★

1 cup granulated sugar
6 egg yolks
1 tablespoon vanilla
1 quart heavy cream

Thoroughly combine the sugar, yolks, and vanilla in a stainless steel bowl.

Pour the cream into a saucepan and bring to a boil, then add slowly to the egg mixture in the bowl, whisking constantly.

Return the mixture to the saucepan and heat, stirring constantly to prevent burning. When the mixture just starts to boil, remove the pan immediately from the heat and return the mixture to the stainless steel bowl, placed in an ice bath.

Continue stirring the mixture so that it cools rapidly. When the temperature drops to about 75°, refrigerate the sauce until it's needed. It will thicken as it cools. If it becomes too thick, slowly add small quantities of milk to adjust it to the desired consistency.

Place a serving of the bread pudding on a dessert plate and spoon crème anglaise over the top. Garnish as desired.

Inspired by the afternoon performance, a visitor might while away an hour or more learning a few basic *hula* movements at the Wallace Dance Studio adjacent to the Royal Hawaiian's Surf Room.

Surf Room bar.

Surf Room cocktail menu.

The Royal Grounds

To the existing abundant native growth, including many two-hundred-year-old coconut palms in the Coconut Grove, landscape designer R. T. Stevens added thousands of plants—hibiscus, ferns, red bougainvillea, poinciana, ti, monkeypod, taro, crotons, banana, banyan, papaya, and other flora—to create a tropical storybook setting across the twelve acres of Royal Hawaiian grounds bordering the white sands of Waikiki. Beyond the beach were the Pacific's infinite shades of blue and, to the southeast, the drama of Diamond Head. Fragrant breezes drifted through the palms, whispering tales of tropical romance to lovers on the *lanais*. Outdoors in the gardens, guests strolled, read, rested, watched young men climb the coconut trees, or attended performances of historical pageants.

Coconut tree climbers in the Royal Hawaiian gardens.

Harry Thiele (right) and friend at the
Royal Hawaiian beer garden.

The Coconut Grove Bar was converted to
a soda fountain during the war.

Rest and Relaxation

Following the attack on Pearl Harbor on December 7, 1941, the Navy Recreation and Morale Office leased the Royal Hawaiian Hotel and put it into operation as a Rest and Relaxation facility for the U.S. military. For the duration of the war, the Royal did not offer accommodations to the general public. (The Moana was the only major hotel in Honolulu that continued normal guest hotel operations; however, it was always filled to capacity, generally with service personnel.) At the Royal, officers paid a dollar per day for a room, and enlisted men paid twenty-five cents, with three or four men to a room. The average stay for a sailor was ten days. The world-famous Coconut Grove Bar served as a soda fountain, and alcohol service apparently was moved outdoors, where a beer garden was frequented by enlisted men.

At the beginning of the war, the only door to the wine cellar in the Royal's basement had been mortared up to make it look like part of the foundation. During the postwar refurbishment, two days of jackhammering were required to break through two feet of concrete to liberate the enormous stores of wine, liquor, and champagne, all intact and ready to delight the palates of the Royal's guests.

Renovations of the Royal Hawaiian following World War II totaled two million dollars and lasted one year. The reopening party took place on February 1, 1947, exactly twenty years after the original opening.

Sailors on R&R.

THE ROYAL HAWAIIAN

~~~~ on the beach at Waikiki

Announcing The Reopening of the

ROYAL HAWAIIAN HOTEL *Honolulu, Hawaii*

After five years of service to the Armed Forces the Royal Hawaiian Hotel will reopen *February 1, 1947*.
It reopens to enter a new era. In the beauty of its famous Waikiki beach setting...
in its traditional hospitality...in the gaiety which found unique expression in "dancing under the stars"
...in all the charm of atmosphere which gave it such high place in the travel world...it will again be
the Royal Hawaiian. But in furnishings...in decoration and appointments...in complete modernization
throughout, it will be a new Royal Hawaiian...with greater beauty and finer service than ever...assured
of new eminence among the great hotels of the world.

WARREN B. PINNEY, *Managing Director*

THE MOANA HOTEL:
"THE FIRST LADY OF WAIKIKI"

In 1928, Matson Navigation Company acquired the Moana Hotel. Erected twenty-seven years before, the Moana was the first hotel on Waikiki Beach and was known to locals and tourists alike as "the First Lady of Waikiki."

Among Polynesians, the word "*Moana*" translates to "broad expanse of the ocean," a fitting name for a hotel situated at the brink of the Pacific. The site where the Moana stands once was called "*Ulukou*," and was a sacred compound for Oahu's highest ranking chiefs. A century before the Moana Hotel was built, Kamehameha the Great had made his home on this spot.

In the mid-1890s, well-known architect and designer Oliver G. Traphagen was commissioned to create a beachside hotel on the Walter C. Peacock estate at Waikiki, by renovating the existing home and adding guest cottages. The plans evolved over the course of several years until construction began in 1899, under the auspices of Peacock's Moana Hotel Company, Ltd. Traphagen's elaborate design incorporated elements of Arts and Crafts, beaux arts, Queen Anne, Georgian revival, and neoclassical motifs into the predominantly colonial structure. At just four stories high, the new hotel was one of the island's tallest buildings.

The elegant Moana Hotel, circa 1910.

Moana brochures.

DINNER

Canape, Regind

SOUPS

Consomme with Rice

Cream of Cauliflower

RELISHES

Chow Chow   Radishes   Olives

FISH

Fillet of Red Snapper, Morney

Pomme Naturelle

ENTREES

Sweetbread Croquette, Green Peas

Queen Fritters

Punch, Romaine

ROAST

Prime Ribs of Beef au Jus

Roast Duck, Apple Sauce

Mashed Potatoes   New Potatoes in Cream

Stewed Celery   String Beans

SALAD

Lettuce and Tomatoes   Asparagus, Mayonnaise

DESSERT

Chocolate Pudding, Vanilla Sauce

Vanilla Ice Cream   Assorted Cakes

Fruits in Season   Mixed Nuts

Cheese

Cafe Noir

BREAKFAST 7 TO 10   LUNCH 12 TO 2   DINNER 6 TO 8.

OUR DRINKING WATER IS FROM OUR OWN ARTESIAN WELL.

Sunday, March 14, 1920.

Moana Hotel dinner menu, 1920.

Moana Hotel.

A Grand Opening for a Grand Lady

The Moana Hotel opened on March 11, 1901, with an elaborate dinner and entertainment. Guests were escorted to a dining room and dance floor that extended out over the ocean. The tables were set with pure white linens and fine colonial silver, and the booming roll of the Pacific provided a suitable musical background.

The veranda opened out to the Banyan Court.

An early view of the dining room.

The opening night menu offered all that was delicious and delectable:

California Oyster Cocktail
Consommé in Cups
Cheese Straws
Queen Olives
Salted Almonds
Fillet of English Sole a la Nantu
Sliced Cucumbers
Pommes Dauphin
Stewed Terrapin a la Maryland, en Caessa
Larded Tenderloin of Beef a la Portuguese
Choice Island Asparagus with Sauce Hollandaise
Punch a la Romaine
Roast Mallard Duck au Cressau
Sara Potatoes
Neapolitan Ice Cream
Assorted Cakes
Roquefort Cheese
Toasted Crackers
Café Noir
Cigar

In addition to the oceanside dining room and dance floor, Moana's public areas boasted a library, billiard parlor, ladies' parlor, and a lavish rooftop garden observatory offering 360-degree views of Honolulu. Footsteps in the spacious halls were cushioned by plush carpets, and the open, airy rooms were appointed with finely crafted chairs and writing tables. The territory's first electric-powered elevator carried guests from the lobby to the floors above.

Guest room interior, 1915.

Guest room interior, 1950.

The Moana cottages.

Guest Rooms

Each of the Moana's original seventy-five guest rooms had its own telephone and adjoining bathroom; these were unheard-of luxuries in that era. Brass bedsteads were complemented by colonial furnishings.

Two wings added in 1918 combined with the original hotel structure to form an H-shaped complex. The wings and the addition of two floors increased the number of guest rooms to 275. The Moana also offered its guests several homelike cottages that were located directly across the street from the hotel, sometimes referred as the "Seaside Hotel."

In the 1930s, a surprising number of people had the means to travel in style and elegance, despite the economic depression that followed the 1929 stock market crash. During that era, rates at the elegant and exclusive Moana Hotel were:

European Plan   Single: $4, $5, and $6 per day
(without meals)   Double: $6, $8, and $10 per day

American Plan   Single: $6, $7, and $8 per day
(with meals)   Double: $11, 13, and $15 per day

On the American plan, guests were treated to delicious and beautifully presented dishes that they would not soon forget. Prominent among these was one of the world's favorite desserts, Cherries Jubilee.

THE *Banyan Tree will tell you the Story*

Make friends with the old Banyan Tree in the court of the Moana. It will whisper the names of many a world-known personage who has sat beneath its boughs. It will make a thousand gay scenes re-live. And pride will rustle its leaves as it speaks of the number of people it has welcomed to the hospitality of the Moana. Privileges include those of the Waialae Golf Course. And pleasures include everything for which Waikiki is famous.

Accommodations include cottages in the hotel gardens of four to ten rooms. *Daily Rates:* For Hotel or Cottages, from $6 double, $7 single, per person, American plan.

MOANA
AT WAIKIKI

A. Benaglia, Managing Director

Ad for the Moana Hotel, 1939.

Moana's Cherries Jubilee ★

Executive chef Daniel Delbrel still serves this classic dessert in the Ship's Tavern restaurant at the Sheraton Moana Surfrider.

SERVES 4
1/2 teaspoon cinnamon
1/4 cup sugar
1 can black pitted cherries
2 thin lemon slices
1/2 cup brandy
Choice of ice cream, or purchased or homemade sponge cake

Mix the cinnamon and sugar together and set aside.

Heat the cherries and their juice in a pan along with the lemon slices. Sprinkle the cinnamon-sugar mixture into the pan.

In a separate saucepan, heat the brandy slightly. Reserve one large spoonful of heated brandy, and add the rest to the cherries. Set the spoonful of brandy ablaze, then add to cherries. When the flame dies down, fan it out and serve at once over ice cream or sponge cake.

Moana Hotel stationery.

The Moana Pier

Shortly before the Moana Hotel was first proposed in the 1890s, a pier had been built, extending out over the water. It became known locally as the Moana Pier, a popular place where couples went for a stroll to watch the moon rise above the ocean. At the pier's far end was a small pavilion where amateur musicians gathered informally, drawing locals and tourists alike.

"There was a long pier which jutted out into the ocean with a square pavilion at the end. Here the tourists and townspeople gathered to hear the beach boys strumming on their ukuleles and guitars under a full moon. I could still go back to those vivid memories of those perfect nights with the moon shining down on an almost flat sea with the splash of a tiny wave feeling its way onto the beach. Lovers strolled under the spell of moonlight that only Hawai'i can produce."

—Art Wyeth, in "As I Remember"

In the early 1930s, the Board of Harbor Commissioners declared the pier unsafe, and it was demolished. This fact was quietly observed in an issue of *Paradise of the Pacific* magazine: "The old Moana Pier, on which a thousand romances have begun and perhaps as many dissolved, has been torn down."

THE LAST DECADE: THE SURFRIDER AND PRINCESS KAIULANI HOTELS

With Matson luxury liners back in service between the mainland and Honolulu following World War II, more and more tourists were flocking to Hawai'i and increasing the demand for accommodations. In 1951, Matson responded by constructing the eight-story, 152-room Surfrider. Designed by San Francisco architect Gardner A. Dailey, the new Surfrider was connected with the Moana Hotel on the ground floor. The new hotel's guests registered in the lobby of the Moana, and could take their meals in the Moana's dining rooms, as well.

The Surfrider Hotel's main entry.

The Surfrider Hotel.

The Surfrider's lounge.

Surfrider guest room and view of the Pacific.

Surfrider guest room.

Eventually the Moana and the Surfrider, along with a new Surfrider Tower, were combined to form a complex that today is known as the Sheraton Moana Surfrider Resort.

The grand opening of the elegant Princess Kaiulani Hotel on June 11, 1955—King Kamehameha Day—was heralded by the blowing of conch shells, a tradition on important occasions in ancient Hawai'i. More than one hundred invited guests, including Matson officials, gathered on the terrace near the Orchid Pool for the ceremony, which began at the stroke of noon. Two *kahilis* were placed on either side of a near life-size portrait of Princess Kaiulani (by Honolulu artist Lloyd Sexton) when the painting was dedicated in the main lobby following a *lei* ceremony.

Surf Rider HOTEL

ON THE BEACH AT WAIKIKI
Honolulu, Hawaii

RATE SCHEDULE
1957-1958

The Princess Kaiulani Hotel.

Princess Kaiulani guest room.

The Princess Kaiulani's décor featured
ancient island images and icons.

The hotel was named for Victoria Kaiulani, a Hawaiian
princess whose father was Governor A. S. Cleghorn. *Kaiulani* means "the royal sacred one." Robert Louis Stevenson
befriended Princess Kaiulani and wrote a farewell poem in
her autograph book in 1889 before she left for school in
England:

> Forth from her land to mine she goes,
> The Island maid, the Island rose,
> Light of heart and bright of face,
> The daughter of a double race.
>
> Her Islands here in Southern sun
> Shall mourn their Kaiulani gone.
> And I, in her dear banyan's shade,
> Look vainly for my little maid.

Ocean view from a Princess Kaiulani guest room.

But our Scots Islands far away.
Shall glitter with unwonted day,
And cast for once their tempest by
To smile in Kaiulani's eye.

Princess Kaiulani and Stevenson never met again.

Situated on the south edge of the former Ainahau
Estate, where the Moana-Seaside cottages had been located,
the Princess Kaiulani was built by Matson to handle the
ever-increasing tourist trade. At eleven stories, rising 131 feet
above street level, the Princess Kaiulani Hotel was the tallest
hotel to be built in Hawai'i since the Royal Hawaiian. It was
erected by Pacific Construction Company. The original
hotel was modern Polynesian in design, its terrazzo floors
in a *tapa* (treebark paper) motif, columns paneled in

Portrait of Princess Victoria Kaiulani (1875–1899), painted by
Honolulu artist Lloyd Sexton and presented at the time of the
hotel opening in 1955.

golden Philippine mahogany, furniture framed of *koa* wood and upholstered in bright fabrics. The entire eleventh floor opened onto a wide promenade on three sides, offering a panoramic view of Honolulu, Waikiki, Diamond Head, and the Pacific Ocean.

The Princess Kaiulani was the last Matson hotel to be built on Waikiki. In 1959, Matson Navigation Company divested all of its non-shipping assets, selling its Waikiki

Poolside at the Princess Kaiulani.

hotels to the Sheraton Corporation. Matson historian Fred Stindt reflected, "The sale saddened the hearts of many. The hotels had become a part of the Grand Manner of Matson."

The S.S. *Lurline*'s former chief steward, Jack Abramson, knew Waikiki during those great years when it was more sand than high-rise, and when Matson's Moana and Royal Hawaiian seemed to tower over Waikiki:

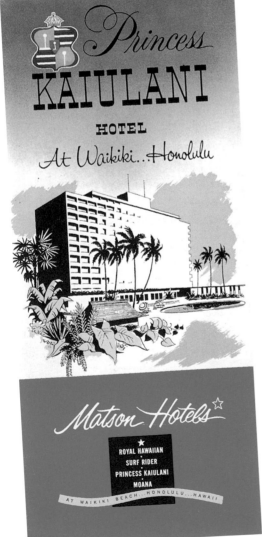

Princess Kaiulani Hotel brochure.

I loved it then and I love it now, but I miss what it was like then. I'm just glad I knew what it once was, so peaceful and quiet.

—Jack Abramson

Paradise Found

*T*he palace of an ancient Hawaiian king had for its ceiling the blue dome of the skies . . . for its pillars and walls the palms and lush foliage of the tropics. Striking symbols of his dominance were his brilliant feather cloak and helmet that he wore on state occasions. Wherever he appeared in state, attendants bore the picturesque cylinder-shaped feather *kahilis*. Their awe of the king could not suppress the Hawaiians' natural love of merry-making. Royalty gave it free expression. *Hula* dancing to chanted music and the pounding of gourds, lively games, horsemanship, sports of the sea, and always a well-provisioned, flower-decked *luau*.

Pomp and Circumstance by Eugene Savage.

THE ROYAL HAWAIIAN *LUAU*

Carried to the islands by the great ship *Lurline*, and settled in their rooms at one of Matson's Waikiki hotels, vacationers now turned their attention to exploring and enjoying the Hawaiian experience.

Nearly everyone who vacationed in Honolulu went to at least one *luau*. Many had their first such experience at the Royal Hawaiian Hotel's weekly *luau*, hosted at sunset on the Ocean Lawn.

Luau-goers were greeted with *alohas* and *leis*, then sipped tropical drinks and enjoyed a breathtaking view of Waikiki and Diamond Head. Hawaiian music, chanting, and *hula* dancing were followed by the serving of the *Kalua* pig (traditionally roasted in an underground pit called an *imu*). The bountiful meal, featuring dishes the mainlanders had never tasted before, was properly eaten with the fingers rather than utensils. Following the meal, the hotel's spectacular Royal Polynesian Extravaganza of music and dance was performed under the stars.

Luaus are carefully choreographed affairs, steeped in age-old Polynesian tradition. Typically held outdoors, preferably on a palm-fringed tropical beach, they feature bounty gleaned from nature— ferns, sweet potatoes, and coconut milk from the land . . . and . . . fish from the sea. . . . Enhanced by the sound of lilting guitars, soft Hawaiian songs, and the *hula*, few experiences can match the *luau* as a romantic mood setter.

—Royal Hawaiian Hotel Press Kit

The Authentic Royal Hawaiian Mai Tai Bar's Mai Tai ★

In 1953, the Royal Hawaiian Hotel engaged Victor ("Trader Vic") Bergeron to set up an outdoor drinking establishment near the beach. Dubbed the "Mai Tai Bar," it gave a home to the popular tropical drink of the same name.

The mai tai served there is garnished not just with a paper umbrella but also with a stick of sugar cane, a fresh mint leaf, a wedge of pineapple, and a fresh orchid.

SERVES 4

Mai Tai Mix
2 ounces orgeat syrup
2 ounces rock candy syrup
4 ounces orange curaçao
2 ounces sour lemon
10 ounces orange juice

Combine these ingredients in a one-quart measuring cup; add just enough water to total one quart.

For each serving:

5 ounces Mai Tai Mix (above)
1 ounce white rum
1 ounce Myers's dark rum

Fill a mai tai glass (short tumbler) with ice. Pour in the Mai Tai Mix and white rum. Float the dark rum on top. Garnish as desired.

Man pounding *poi*.

Poi ★

A vital element of the traditional Hawaiian diet, *poi* is made from the corm (root) of the *taro*. This tropical root crop has been grown since early times. *Poi* is easily digested and a good source of B vitamins, calcium, and phosphorus.

To make *poi*, pound cooked and peeled *taro* corms and add water until the *poi* is of the desired consistency. Some people allow it to ferment, so that it develops a sour, tangy flavor.

THE ROYAL HAWAIIAN'S TRADITIONAL *LUAU* MENU

Kalua Pig	Fried Rice
Teriyaki Steak	Baked Sweet Potatoes
Mahimahi	Fresh Pineapple
Lomilomi Salmon	Sliced Fresh Fruits
Laulau	Haupia
Chicken Long Rice	Banana Bread
Poi	Coconut Cake

Luau-goers tasting two-finger *poi*.

MUSIC AND ENTERTAINMENT

Music and entertainment were important elements of Matson's Grand Manner, not only aboard ship, but also at the Waikiki hotels. In the 1930s, both the Royal Hawaiian Band and the Moana orchestra were led by Johnny Noble—composer of "Hula Blues." In 1934, Harry Owens took over as leader of the Royal Hawaiian Band, freeing Noble to book entertainment for both hotels.

Lobby card from the movie *Waikiki Wedding*.

Harry Owens ★

In 1934, Owens wrote "Sweet Leilani" for his daughter the day after she was born. Bing Crosby sang the song in the film *Waikiki Wedding*.

Harry Owens, Director of the famous Royal Hawaiian Hotel Orchestra, and his tiny daughter, "Sweet Leilani."

Harry Owens with daughter Leilani.

Harry Owens with the Royal Hawaiian Band and *hula* dancers.

Entertainers at the Royal included Al Kealoha Perry and his Hawaiian orchestra and singers, the Royal Hawaiian Band with vocalists the Hawaiian Serenaders, the Royal Hawaiian Girls Glee Club, and the "Beach Boy" musicians.

Special programs seemed to follow in the wake of the *Lurline*'s comings and goings. Each *Lurline*-load of guests was welcomed with a *Malihini* Party at the Princess Kaiulani Hotel, offering the new-comers a Hawaiian buffet followed by international music and entertainment. Within forty-eight hours they were considered honorary citizens and fêted at *Kama'aina* Night at the Royal Hawaiian Hotel. On nights before the ship departed, the Moana Hotel hosted an *Aloha* Party—another elegant meal and dancing under the Banyan Tree.

Mrs. Clara Inter was famous at Waikiki. Dressed in a colorful *muumuu* and a hat, she took on the beloved persona of Hilo Hattie, and bowled over audiences with her very unique—and funny!—take on *hula* and Hawaiian music.

Al Kealoha Perry and his Hawaiian orchestra and singers in 1947.

Regular entertainers in and around the Royal Hawaiian Hotel were the Royal Hawaiian Girls Glee Club and the original "Beach Boys."

for your pleasure

MATSON HOTEL EVENTS

May 11 to May 17, 1958

Malihini Night

Orchid Pool — Princess Kaiulani Hotel

Here is your gayest introduction to Hawaii! Given at the Princess Kaiulani Hotel where you'll meet international music and entertainment — from Waikiki, from China, from Portugal, from Samoa . . . and enjoy a bountiful Hawaiian buffet. Every ship arrival night.

$5.25 Tax Incl.

ROYAL
HAWAIIAN
❋
SURFRIDER
❋
PRINCESS
KAIULANI
❋
MOANA

At Waikiki Beach
Honolulu, Hawaii

Hoolaulea

This old-style Hawaiian picnic, open to Matson Hotel guests, begins with a scenic ride to Heeia on Windward Oahu. You'll enjoy cocktails on the house, delicious food and hilarious Polynesian entertainment. Fun for all! Social Directors at Matson Hotels will make your reservations. Thursdays.

Events at the Princess Kaiulani, Surfrider, Moana, and Royal Hawaiian.

Johnny Noble and his orchestra.

Hilo Hattie in her bright *muumuu* and funny hat.

When Hilo Hattie does the Hilo Hop,
The folks in Honolulu start to close up shop,
For everything and everybody comes to a stop,
When Hilo Hattie does the Hilo Hop.
　　　—"*Hilo Hattie (Does the Hilo Hop)*,"
　　　　　　　by Don McDiarmid, Sr.

Hilo Hattie was very popular among the tourists who had traveled to the islands aboard the S.S. *Lurline*. But her name and her fame spread far and wide when she became a regular performer on a radio show broadcast from a Waikiki landmark: the Banyan Tree Court at the Moana Hotel.

UNDER THE BANYAN TREE...
HAWAI'I CALLS

An Indian banyan tree was planted at the Moana Hotel in 1904. The old tree still stands, now 75 feet high, with a canopy spreading 150 feet across and a trunk circumference of 40 feet. It is classified technically as "Tree #45" on Hawai'i's Exceptional Tree List, but for anyone who has sat beneath its spreading branches, it is now and always will be "the Banyan Tree at the Moana."

When the Moana Hotel was expanded in 1918, the addition of wings on either side of the original building created a courtyard around the old banyan tree. It was from this courtyard, on July 3, 1935, that Webley Edwards beckoned to a worldwide radio audience for the first time with the words, "From the Banyan Court of the Moana Hotel, overlooking bee-you-tiful Waikiki Beach, it's . . . HAWAI'I CALLS!"

The waves of Waikiki provided the perfect background music for weekly broadcasts of *Hawai'i Calls* from the Moana Hotel. Entertainers on the *lanai* performed not just for the microphone, but for a live crowd gathered beneath the Banyan Tree. The program was created and hosted by Webley Edwards and the title music was composed by Harry Owens and performed by the Royal Hawaiian Band. Alfred Apaka, Andy Bright, Haleloke, Hilo Hattie, Benny Kalama, Gabby Pahinui, Sam Kapu, the Singing Surfriders (the program's "house band"), the Waikiki Girls, and many others were guests on this program destined to become an institution in broadcasting for the next forty years.

As evening flows down out of the misty valleys, and stars hang colored lanterns over Waikiki, or a wide Island moon pours gold between the palms, lights bloom out like sudden flowers on Waikiki Terrace or in the Moana Banyan Court; haunting Hawaiian tunes glide from horns and strings, and smartly attired couples circle in the dance.

—*Polynesian* magazine

Webley Edwards (sitting on the outrigger) with the *Hawai'i Calls* troupe, November 1954.

Banyan Court at the Moana.

Moana Banyan Tree Punch ⭐

The Moana no longer serves this cocktail, but the recipe survives in the hotel's archives. Its blend of flavors must have been the perfect libation to sip while sitting 'neath the Banyan Tree listening to the strains of *Hawai'i Calls*.

SERVES 1
1 1/2 ounces rum
1/2 ounce lime juice
1 teaspoon grenadine
1 ounce pineapple juice
1/2 ounce guava juice

Pour all the ingredients into large mixing glass filled with shaved ice. Stir well and serve decorated with a vanda orchid.

LOOK WHO STAYED AT MATSON'S HOTELS

Matson's hotels at Waikiki were frequented by the rich and famous. Over the years, hundreds of celebrities from the worlds of entertainment, finance, and politics signed the guest registers. In the heyday of steamship travel to the islands they included:

Gracie Allen and
   George Burns
Clark Andrews and
   Claire Trevor
Lucille Ball
Mr. and Mrs. Jack Benny
Edgar Bergen and
   Charlie McCarthy
George Brent
Eddie Cantor
Walter P. Chrysler
Broderick Crawford
Bing Crosby
Joe DiMaggio
The Duponts
Amelia Earhart Putnam
Douglas Fairbanks
Henry and Anne
   McDonnell Ford
Clark Gable and
   Lady Sylvia Ashley
The Gettys
Al Jolson and Ruby Keeler
Henry J. Kaiser

Boris Karloff
Peter Lawford
Carole Lombard and
   William Powell
Alice Roosevelt Longworth
Jeanette MacDonald and
   Gene Raymond
Lord Mountbatten
The Mellons
Mary Pickford and
   Buddy Rogers
The Prince of Wales
Nelson and Mary Todhunter
   Clark Rockefeller
Will Rogers
Gilbert Roland
Frank Sinatra
Norma Talmadge
Shirley Temple
Mr. and Mrs. Spencer Tracy
Deborah Walley
Esther Williams
Loretta Young

Clark Andrews and Claire Trevor.

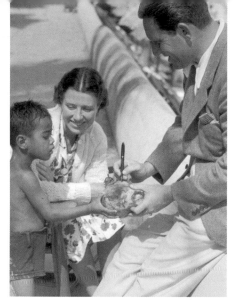

Spencer Tracy signing his autograph.

Bing Crosby auditioned *hula* girls for *Waikiki Wedding*.

Edgar Bergen with Charley and Mortimer.

Matson's Mary Pickford Cocktail ★

With a nod to screen star Mary Pickford, we include her namesake recipe, from a March 1934 memo to Matson stewards.

SERVES 1
¹/₄ jigger pineapple juice
¹/₄ jigger grenadine
¹/₂ jigger Bacardi rum

Shake well and pour over ice in a short tumbler.

Mary Pickford, "America's Sweetheart," and her husband Buddy Rogers on their honeymoon in 1937.

ALL IN A DAY'S PLAY

The Royal Hawaiian and Moana Hotels had a reciprocal arrangement so that guests staying at one hotel were privileged to all activities at the other. This allowed guests of both hotels to enjoy a wide range of entertainment, dances, amusements, sports (including archery, tennis, badminton, lawn bowling, lawn and paddle tennis, a putting green, sailing, and horseback riding), and even *hula* lessons. This tradition of sharing amenities extended to nearby Waialae Golf Course, which Seth Raynor had designed so that every hole was a reproduction from one of the world's most renowned courses: St. Andrews, Prestwick, North Berwick, National, Piping Rock, Valido.

Regardless of which hotel one was staying in, the main attraction was the beach. Many vacationers eagerly anticipated the luxury of relaxing all day, carefree, the Pacific lapping gently at the shore. As long as tourists have been going to Honolulu, this vision has found its reality in that stretch of white sand known as Waikiki.

Tourists marveled at the perfect air and water temperatures, and were both surprised and charmed when they discovered that the Hawaiian language has no equivalent term for the word "weather." Honolulu's temperatures occasionally dipped to 55 degrees or spiked to as much as 88 degrees, but generally hovered comfortably and reliably in the 70s. Add perfect water temperatures—an almost constant 78 degrees—and it's no wonder Waikiki was called "the beach that knows no winter."

Brochures promised fun in the surf.

Mickey Rooney on the tennis courts at the Royal Hawaiian.

This little piece of heaven offered more than a comfy horizontal surface on which to recline and observe the movement of sun and clouds over Diamond Head. Matson Navigation Company's Waikiki Beach hotels provided their guests with cushions, towels, umbrellas, chairs, and the personal services of beach attendants. And anyone so inclined could rent an outrigger canoe or jump right into some of the world's best surfing. Lessons in both sports were offered to Matson hotel guests.

Waialae Golf Course.

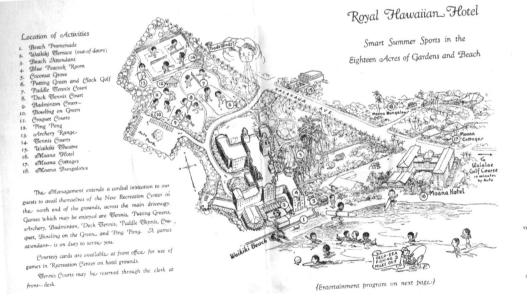

Location of Activities
1. Beach Promenade
2. Waikiki Terrace (out-of-doors)
3. Beach Attendant
4. Blue Peacock Room
5. Coconut Grove
6. Putting Green and Clock Golf
7. Paddle Tennis Court
8. Deck Tennis Court
9. Badminton Courts
10. Bowling on Green
11. Croquet Courts
12. Ping Pong
13. Archery Range
14. Tennis Courts
15. Waikiki Theatre
16. Moana Hotel
17. Moana Cottages
18. Moana Bungalows

The Management extends a cordial invitation to our guests to avail themselves of the New Recreation Center in the north end of the grounds, across the main driveway. Games which may be enjoyed are Tennis, Putting Greens, Archery, Badminton, Deck Tennis, Paddle Tennis, Croquet, Bowling on the Green, and Ping Pong. A games attendant is on duty to serve you.

Courtesy cards are available at front office for use of games in Recreation Center on hotel grounds.

Tennis Courts may be reserved through the clerk at front desk.

Royal Hawaiian Hotel

Smart Summer Sports in the
Eighteen Acres of Gardens and Beach

{Entertainment program on next page}

Location of activities for both Moana and Royal hotel guests, and entertainment schedule, November 30–December 6, 1941.

FRIDAY
DEC. 5

8:30 P. M. HAWAIIAN CONCERT on the Waikiki Terrace
The Honolulu Serenaders
American plan guests may obtain complimentary guest cards at the front office of the Royal Hawaiian Hotel for the dance at the Moana Hotel

SATURDAY
DEC. 6

8:30 P. M. DANCING ON THE WAIKIKI TERRACE
Giggie Royse and His Orchestra
Kaalon Notley in Modern Hulas
The Aloha Maids
Boleyn - Anderson Studio Present Modern Dances

(SUBJECT TO CHANGE)

Royal Hawaiian Hotel
Moana Hotel
Waialae Golf Club

Weekly Program of Entertainment
November 30 to December 6, 1941

Sports and Recreation

Waikiki Beach.

Spencer Tracy and Eddie Cantor with Lt. Col. Frank Hayes.

The contours of Waikiki's outer reefs combined with the influence of the trade winds to create ideal surf conditions that made these waters a mecca for the world's surfboarding enthusiasts and outrigging buffs. Here generations of Hawaiian chiefs and kings had originated surfing and outrigging, practicing them for centuries and establishing them as the islands' essential sports, vital to the royal tradition of balancing hard work with equally hard play.

> It is a never-ending thrill just to watch [them] come soaring in, standing erect on the narrow, rushing boards, keeping balance with superb skill on the moving face of the water—and beside them, the hollow log canoes, filled with happy, shouting passengers, plunging toboggan-like down the advancing slope of the same wave.
> —*Polynesian* magazine, 1939

Waikiki's most famous surfer, Duke Kahanamoku, grew up spending more time in the water than out of it. Competing in Olympic games from 1912 until 1932, he earned a total of six medals—three gold, two silver, and one bronze—in swimming events. But locally he was equally well known for his surfing feats. A familiar figure around Waikiki Beach, he posed with hundreds—perhaps thousands—of tourists who wanted to have their photo taken with "the Duke." He eventually became sheriff of Honolulu and escorted numerous celebrity visitors, earning the moniker "Ambassador of *Aloha.*"

Among the travelers who disembarked from the *Lurline* were a certain number of serious game fishermen. They came not only from the mainland, but from all over the world, to try their hand at Hawai'i's waters. Here the fishing was outstanding—tuna, swordfish, or marlin—and whether the fisherman was a regular guy or a world-famous celebrity, a prize catch was followed by the ritual of spinning fish stories.

Nabbing a fifty-five pound *mahimahi* gave Bing Crosby something to croon about.

The Moana and the Royal Hawaiian Hotels shared amenities so that guests at one hotel could enjoy activities at both.

Waikiki surfers, including "Duke" Kahanamoku.

Matson ad, 1939.

ISLAND SOUVENIRS

Everywhere they went, the tourists longed to take home a bit of what they were experiencing. They had a multitude of shops to explore throughout the islands, or they might have found the perfect memento right in the Royal Hawaiian Hotel's arcade, location of the Hawai'i & South Seas Curio Company—recognized as "the world's largest Pacific souvenir store."

Favorite souvenirs included Polynesian crafts such as *lau hala* (pandanus leaf) place mats and wall decorations, bowls and trays made of *koa* and monkeypod, calabashes, *aloha* shirts, *muumuus*, shawls, handmade *ukuleles*, jade, Chinese rugs, and Hawaiian etchings.

Souvenir shops offered a myriad of treasures.

Souvenir postcards.

A Matson ad featured popular souvenir items *koa* bowls and *leis*.

Souvenir brochures, pamphlets, booklets, and matchbooks.

Ellen Greive in the late 1920s, modeling a *tapa* cloth vest. *Tapa* garments were bought by many tourists visiting the islands.

Souvenirs made by island craftsmen were especially treasured.

Matson's shipboard publication, *Polynesian*, suggested, "A souvenir should be a thing of delight itself, something that combines the charm of the place or experience it recalls with a charm of its own." Something to wear—clothing or a shell necklace—in an island motif was both useful and a reminder of a place that held many happy memories.

A California artist and designer named Ellen Greive created jackets, vests, belts, collars and cuffs from *tapa*, a form of paper made by pounding bark of the *wauke* (paper mulberry tree).

On the other hand, a traveler might imbue some otherwise insignificant item with sentiment. Perhaps she saved a cocktail napkin from the mai tai bar, where she had chatted with a handsome stranger and lingered over a second drink before kissing him goodbye; the point of tucking the napkin first into her pocket, then into a scrapbook or jewelry box, was to hold on to something tangible, no matter how humble. Its logo or its subtle hue could still evoke, years later, a memory of that fascinating man with the moustache and the sea-green eyes.

Besides selecting souvenirs for themselves, travelers also sought gifts for friends back home. They often chose island fruit (not so readily available on the mainland as it is today). A visit to the Dole Cannery might convince them that fresh pineapple was just the thing. Tourists took home crates of fresh pineapple—"the king of fruits"—and Matson provided refrigeration on the return trip. Or a drive around the island might present an opportunity to simply climb up on top of the car and pluck a bunch of bananas, free for the taking. Coconuts also had their charms, not the least of which was that they were easy to pack (an advantage that also held true for macadamia nuts and bags of Kona coffee beans). Coconuts also could be addressed and mailed through the U.S. Postal Service, unwrapped, making a much bigger impression than a "wish-you-were-here" postcard.

Unconventional visit to a pineapple field.

Picking bananas from a car rooftop.

Pineapple was a tasty souvenir.

Love's Hawaiian Fruitcakes were a favorite any time of year, and Munro Ltd. jams and jellies could be shipped or carried back to the mainland with no fear of spoilage.

Many visitors were captivated by both the flavor and the scent of ginger. The native plant—'awapuhi—grows to a height of one or two feet and bears a pale yellow blossom. In *Natural History of Hawaii* William Alanson Bryan wrote that the ginger's juice "was used by the beauty doctors of a former time as a dressing for the hair, and was found on the dressing table of the Hawaiian belle." The fragrance of ginger was delightful, but the blooms were fragile, so mainlanders were more likely to bring its bounty home in the form of "Hawaiian Dry Ginger Ale," formulated by Walter Rycroft, who also developed "Rycroft Hawaiian Pineapple Dry."

A cache of souvenirs sometimes included a photo or menu autographed by some celebrity or other. And, of course, celebrities must have their own souvenirs, as well.

But finally, eventually, inevitably, our happy travelers' time in Hawai'i drew to an end. Sadly, even tearfully, they stowed the newly purchased souvenirs among their clothes as they packed their bags and trunks. No matter how happy they would be to return to family and friends, no matter how true it is that there's no place like home, a part of them would remain forever in the islands.

Kanikapila!
(Strike up the band.—Sort of a "whoopee" shout.)

ROYAL HAWAIIAN PINEAPPLE COCKTAIL

1 jigger gin
1 jigger pineapple juice
⅓ jigger lime juice
1 tsp. Cointreaux

Add ice to this recipe, also. Shake well and serve in a fresh pineapple cut off across the top.

Typically South Sea in atmosphere, is the Halekulani Hotel which snuggles beneath a grove of rustling palms beside the beach at Waikiki. This charming inn makes a cocktail known the world over.

"Today we serve cocktails in the Halekulani bar only," says Mr. Richard Kimball, the energetic young hotel manager. "But before the war we had a custom of serving drinks outside on the Coral Lanai beside the sea wall. It was a pleasant spot to relax and watch the sun dip into the sea behind Waianae, or wait for the moon to come up back of Koko Head. The Halekulani Cocktail was the popular drink in those days. Masa, our bartender, however, has originated a mixture which he calls Waikiki Cocktail. At the moment this drink is number one on the hit parade."

Good gin, rum and beer are produced in Hawaii.

18

Hawaiian Hospitality booklet, Dole Pineapple Company, 1944.

Like any other youngster, Shirley Temple could spend endless hours looking for—and finding—treasures that had washed ashore. Here she photographed a playmate with her trove of glass floats (commonly woven into fishing nets to keep them from sinking).

Goodbye, Honolulu

*T*he time had come to return home. Travelers' hearts were full as once again they heard *"Aloha Oe,"* this time sung as a farewell rather than a greeting. They waved at loved ones on the dock, but now were waving goodbye rather than hello. *Leis* adorned them, but soon they would toss them over *Lurline's* railing, signifying their trust that if the *leis* washed back to shore, they too would return to Hawai'i.

The S.S. *Lurline* passing Diamond Head.

SAILING DAY

Leaving Hawai'i was a bittersweet thing. It was sad to leave behind so many wonderful experiences, but what great fortune it was to have been here: the trade winds, fragrant *leis*, sun sparkling on ocean waves, flashing smiles of swaying *hula* girls, warm sand, luscious *luaus*, sounds of surf mingling with *ukulele* and steel guitar. Those boarding the S.S. *Lurline* were loathe to step on the gangplank—fittingly called "the bridge of sighs."

The Sailing Day scene at Honolulu's Pier 10 is best described by one who witnessed it many times. William R. Sewell, former chief purser on the S.S. *Lurline*, depicted it in a 1994 article in the *Honolulu Advertiser*:

> Farewell parties were legendary on board the Matson ships. The lavish food, the freely flowing drinks, the flower *leis*, the music and everyone dancing, the sobbing when sweethearts had to part at sailing time. The parties began early and ended as the gangplank was raised. I was always amazed at the large number of arriving passengers who would return the same afternoon to say, "Farewell, *aloha*" to the ship, its passengers, and crew. A bond had been created! When the ship's whistle sounded, every heart skipped a beat and the tempo accelerated. One long blast at thirty minutes prior to sailing time, two long blasts at fifteen minutes, and three long mournful blasts as the hawsers were tossed from their capstans. The ship moved, streamers broke, and the brass horns of the Royal Hawaiian Band struck up *"Aloha Oe."* People wept openly. I made over 110 crossings and every departure tugged at my heart strings as if it were the first Boat Day.

Counter sales girls in Matson's Honolulu ticket office booked passengers headed for the mainland from Hawai'i. During *Aloha Week* they dressed in *muumuus* (loose dresses) and *holokus* (long dresses).

Honolulu ticket office.

Leis—one last memento before leaving Hawaii.

YOU CAN'T *Imagine* HAWAII

It's a temptation to describe Hawaii's flowers. But it *isn't possible* because there is no parallel from which to begin. Her flowers defy description, just as *peaceful* Hawaii, reached with *complete safety on American ships,* defies description.

Nevertheless you *can* achieve somewhat of an understanding of her vitality and appeal if you will secure literature *(illustrated)* about HAWAII and CRUISES to the SOUTH SEAS from *Travel Agents* or MATSON LINE offices.

co MATSON NAVIGATION COMPANY
THE OCEANIC STEAMSHIP COMPANY

COPYRIGHT 1940, MATSON NAV. CO.

S. S. LURLINE · S. S. MARIPOSA
S. S. MONTEREY · S. S. MATSONIA

Matson Line TO *Hawaii* · NEW ZEALAND · AUSTRALIA
VIA SAMOA · FIJI

THE LURLINE IS HAWAII

For the finest travel, the LURLINE . . .
for the finest freight service, the
Matson Cargo Fleet . . . to and from Hawaii.

**THEIR LEI-BORNE WISH . . .
TO RETURN SOME DAY**

*. . . speaks in this graceful "Aloha"
to Hawaii as they sail away on the Lurline*

Legend says that if their leis reach the shore, their wish will come true. You, too, have a longfelt wish to see these isles of charming legend and tropic beauty. Make that wish come *supremely* true by sailing on the LURLINE . . . the ship that steeps you in the romance of the sea and crams your voyage with fun, luxury and fine living at no extra cost above your fare. Book round trip and double your travel pleasure . . . *it's twice the fun to sail the LURLINE both ways.*

Matson Lines

See your Travel Agent or any Matson Lines Office: New York, Chicago, San Francisco, Seattle, Portland, Los Angeles, San Diego, Honolulu. And book round trip on the LURLINE.

THE LURLINE SAILS FROM SAN FRANCISCO AND LOS ANGELES ALTERNATELY

Over the years, passengers cultivated the tradition of tossing a *lei* over the ship's railings onto the water—a ritual reminiscent of tossing coins into the Trevi Fountain at Rome—to ensure one's return sometime in the future.

Aloha Oe.
Farewell To Thee.
H.M. QUEEN LILIUOKALANI.

2
Arranged by
ARTHUR LANGE.

Piano

ALOHA OE
FAREWELL TO THEE

COMPOSED BY
H. M. QUEEN
LILIUOKALANI

THE POPULAR MUSIC PUB. CO.
136 N. 9th Street, Phila. Pa.

"Aloha Oe" Lyrics ★

"Aloha Oe" was composed by H.M.
Queen Liliʻuokalani.

Proudly sweeps the rain clouded
    by the cliffs,
As onward it glides through the
    trees,
It seems to be following the *liko*,
The *ahihi lehua* of the vale.

Farewell to thee, farewell to thee,
Thou charming one who dwells
    among the bowers.
One fond embrace before I now
    depart
Until we meet again.

Sad as they were about saying goodbye to Honolulu, the *Lurline*'s passengers had much to look forward to on their return trip to the mainland. On the outbound trip to Hawai'i, shipboard conversations had been full of anticipation about the experiences that lay ahead. Now, with their island stay behind them, acquaintances compared notes about all they'd seen and done. The return voyage was in some ways even pleasanter than the going. One passenger wrote, "There were a lot of people on board we knew, and we were like one big family."

Among the lucky travelers aboard the S.S. *Lurline* on the trip from Honolulu were teenagers setting out from their homes on the islands to go to college on the mainland. In 1930, seventeen-year-old Lillian Adams sailed on a Matson steamship to begin her schooling at the University of California at Berkeley. On that first trip, Adams began a collection of souvenirs—including the Eugene Savage menu covers—which grew as she continued to travel on Matson liners over the years.

> There were a number of us college kids in cabin class. We didn't have the full run of the ship, though. . . . We had some great times. We had dancing every night, . . . and all kinds of activities and games during the day.
>
> —*Lillian Adams*

Speaking of teenagers, the *Lurline* was flooded with them on one of her return trips to the mainland. Former chief steward Jack Abramson reminisced about what he called "the greatest departure": "When Elvis Presley left the island . . . the ship was packed with teenagers and extra security guards had to be assigned to his cabin."

PORTHOLES
Weather conditions sometimes make opening the port decidedly inadvisable. To avoid any possibility of discomfort or injury to your personal effects, call your room steward. He will know when it is practical to open the ports, and for your convenience let him open and close them.

Passengers waving from portholes.

Elvis Presley traveled home on the *Lurline*.

STEAMING HOME ON A FLOATING ISLAND

In the early 1950s, Matson Navigation Company noticed that the *Lurline* was heading home from Hawai'i with up to half of its staterooms empty. With airline service more available and more affordable than ever before, many travelers were opting to fly home so that they could spend the last four days of their vacations on the islands rather than steaming homeward. Matson vice president George F. Hansen came up with an idea: "Let's transform the *Lurline* into a floating ninth island in the Hawaiian archipelago. Then all these vacationers will be in Hawai'i until they step onto the dock in San Francisco or Los Angeles."

An exciting new advertising and promotion campaign urged travelers:

Be sure to book round-trip. Your outbound and homebound trips are two different chapters of the same fascinating story. It's twice the fun to sail the *Lurline* both ways.

Matson ads in the 1950s emphasized round-trip travel.

SAIL WITH THE STARS

GORDON AND SHEILA MacRAE

GOGI GRANT

BILLY DANIELS

Hawaii

LURLINE

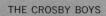

THE CROSBY BOYS

JUNE CHRISTY

DICK CONTINO

STARS AT SEA

To entice return-trip travelers, Matson launched "Sail with the Stars" cruises between Honolulu and the West Coast. The idea was hatched by Seymour Heller in his office above the Brown Derby restaurant on Vine Street in Hollywood. This personal manager to the stars booked his clients for nightclub performances on Matson's luxury liners in the Pacific. Mel Torme, Gordon and Sheila MacRae, Constance Moore, the Crosby Brothers, George Jessel, the Hi-Los and Jaye P. Morgan, Gogi Grant, June Christy, Dick Contino, Billy Daniels, Helen O'Connell, Margaret Whiting, Eva Gabor, and Jimmy Rogers were among those who lured more passengers to travel back to the mainland on the *Lurline* so that they could "Sail with the Stars." Other celebrities who performed aboard the *Lurline* included Dick Shawn, Hilo Hattie, the Mary Kaye Trio, the Eligibles, the Hawaiian Trio, Julie London, Frankie Carle, Vic Damone, and comedian Ben Lessy.

The Hawaiian Trio with Tennessee Ernie Ford. Left to right: Joe Kealoha, Bobby Nichols, Ford, and Pua Kealoha.

Vic Damone.

Sometimes, unexpectedly, celebrities traveling to or from the islands agreed to stand up and sing a tune or shuffle a few steps on the dance floor for the pleasure of the crowd.

On one occasion aboard the *Lurline*, Martin Denny declined to perform in the ballroom, where the stage was too small for his setup. With the help of cruise director David LaKay, arrangements were made for Denny to perform in the screening room, where the tiki décor more nicely showcased Denny's Exotica sound.

The screening room's tiki décor created the perfect environment for a Martin Denny performance.

Martin Denny and his group.

Cruise director Dave LaKay's name badge became a cherished memento of his tenure on the *Lurline*.

The Eligibles.

The Mary Kaye Trio.

THEME NIGHTS

Matson's campaign to increase round-trip bookings inspired the creation of "theme nights" for both outbound and homebound voyages. From that point on, activities and entertainment on the S.S. *Lurline* revolved around a different theme each night, and dinner menus offered dishes fitting the motif of that evening's festivities. As on the outbound trip, theme nights on the homebound trip were great fun for the *Lurline*'s passengers and added a dimension of flavors and experiences like nothing they'd had on the islands. Costumes, parades, special décor, dancing, and music—any detail could be easily arranged, or so the wonderful *Lurline* staff and crew made it look. Anything that was needed always seemed to be at hand, and no idea was too big. Theme nights, like everything else aboard ship, reflected Matson's Grand Manner.

Themes for the first and last evenings at sea were more casual than the others, allowing officers to wear their informal uniforms, as these were especially busy times for the staff and crew.

On some occasions, dinner was followed by "*Le'ale'a* Time," the passengers' own talent show. Many indeed had talent to exhibit: a nice singing voice, proficiency at the piano, mastery on the dance floor. Others were just good sports who, during the day, were run through lighthearted drills in the fine art of can-can or some other performance skill. Matson staff helped participants put costumes together, and of course cocktails were available for any prospective impresario who needed to quell that bothersome bit of stage fright.

David LaKay taught special dances for performances on theme nights. After the scheduled entertainment, passengers who wanted to chime in stood around the piano bar until the wee hours, joining voices in the standards of the day.

Passengers watched *Le'ale'a* Time—the onboard talent competition—as "judge" Joan McKenzie (wife of Captain Robert McKenzie) checked her tally. Sitting in the foreground was the McKenzies' son, Chris.

A LA CLAIRE FONTAINE

Compagnie Générale Transatlantique
French Line

Theme nights featured special menu covers.
This one saluted the French Line.

A little practice, some costumes, and *voila!*
A transformation into can-can dancers.

Bon Voyage Night

The theme for the first night out of Honolulu was Bon Voyage Night. An afternoon dance party brightened up everyone's outlook and reminded them that there were still five days of fun on the return trip. The evening's menu selections featured classic entrees such as *coq au vin* and roasted rack of lamb, finishing with strawberries Romanoff or chocolate soufflé pudding. After dinner, passengers gathered in the ballroom for thirty-cent drinks, games, dances, and prizes.

Polynesian Night

For Polynesian Night, everyone was encouraged to wear the *aloha* shirts, *muumuus*, and *leis* they had purchased in Honolulu. The captain hosted a champagne party, followed by cuisine with an island influence—such as veal cutlet Princess Kapiolani with coconut sauce, roast leg of pork Kalakaua, and guava sherbet—enjoyed amid tropical decorations in the dining rooms. Passengers were treated to Hawaiian entertainment, then participated in a Polynesian fashion show, followed by songs at the piano bar.

Bon Voyage Night menu. A series of covers featuring art by C. Macouillard was used for theme night menus.

MATSON LINES
BON VOYAGE DINNER

Sunday, October 10, 1965

Aboard S.S. LURLINE

Appetizers

Imported Sardines
Fresh Pacific Seafood Cocktail
Assorted Canapes en Bellevue
Fresh Island Papaya
Fruit Cup, Maraschino
Chilled Hawaiian Pineapple

Soups

Consomme Risi-Bisi
Cream of Asparagus
Chilled Vichyssoise

Fish

Fresh Hawaiian Opakapaka Saute, Pistachio Nut Butter, Cole Slaw
Poached Filet of Ling Cod, Mousseline Sauce, Parsley Potatoes

Entrees

Spring Chicken Saute au Burgundy, Onions, Mushrooms with Noodles, Coq au Vin
Center Cut Pork Chop, Sauce Robert, Braised Red Cabbage, Lyonnaise Potatoes
Roasted Rack of Lamb with Mint Sauce, Mixed Vegetables
Garden Fresh Vegetable Platter with Poached Eggs
To Order from Our Charcoal Broiler (Allow Ten Minutes)
Broiled Veal Porterhouse Steak, Sauce, Bordelaise, Hash Brown Potatoes

Roasts

Roast Sirloin of Beef au Jus, Southern Corn Bread, Creamed Horseradish

Vegetables

Baked Banana Squash
Baked Idaho Potato
Brussels Sprouts
O'Brien
Harvard Beets
Lyonnaise
Boiled Carolina Rice
Hashed Brown

Salads

(Dressings of Your Choice)
Hearts of Lettuce
Watercress and Sliced Eggs
Mixed Green
Hawaiian Fruit

Desserts

Strawberries Romanoff
Vanilla Ice Cream
Lemon Cream Roll
Raspberry Sherbet
Angel Food Cake
Chocolate Souffle Pudding
Wine Jello, Chantilly

Cheese

Edam
Liederkranz
Brie
Roquefort
Gouda
Gruyere

Beverages

Coffee
Milk
Sanka
Kona Coffee
Chocolate
Green or Orange Pekoe Tea

Polynesian Night menu.

Papee Mossman on Polynesian Night.

Little Grass Shack ★

Though this simple three-ingredient concoction actually originated decades before Matson instituted its theme nights, it endures as the perfect cocktail for a Polynesian party.

SERVES 1
1/3 jigger pineapple juice
1/3 jigger Cointreau
1/3 jigger gin

Stir and serve in cocktail glass.

"I've Found a Little Grass Skirt for My Little Grass Shack in Hawaii," words and music by Harry Owens and Johnny Noble.

MATSON LINES
Polynesian Night Dinner

Aboard S.S. LURLINE

Appetizers

Crystallized Ginger
Salami-Cheese Cones, Mauna Loa
Fresh Pacific Lobster Cocktail
Lomi Lomi Salmon, Kapiolani

Kumquats in Syrup
Wailohulehu Poi Cocktail
Polynesian Fruit Cup an Grenadine
Iced Passion Fruit au Guava Nectar

Soups

Consomme Prince Kuhio
Japanese Watercress with Tofu
Cold Vichyssoise

Fish

Fried Prawns Tempura, Japanese Style, Hot Soy Sauce, Cucumber Salad
Hawaiian Swordfish Saute, Brown Almond Butter, Straw Potatoes

Entrees

Braised Leg of Pork, Kalakaua, Baked Bananas, Candied Sweet Potatoes, Pineapple
Chinese Chow Mein, Bamboo Shoots, Water Chestnuts, Bean Sprouts, Fried Noodles
Barbecued Fresh Pork Spareribs, Pink Sauce, Fried Rice, Orientale Style
Baked Papaya Stuffed with Lobster Curry, Chutney, Rice Pilaff

To Order from Our Charcoal Broiler (Allow Ten Minutes)
Charcoal Broiled Teriyaki Beef Steak, Sauce Orientale, Long Branch Potatoes

Roasts

Roast Alyesbury Duckling, Apple-Prune Dressing, Sauce Biggarde, Apple Rings

Vegetables

Broccoli, Hollandaise
Baked Idaho Potato
Fresh Carrots, Waikiki
Roast Maunakea
String Beans, Leilani
Candied Sweet Potatoes
Steamed Carolina Rice
Chips

Salads
(Dressings of Your Choice)

Tomato and Avocado
Manoa Lettuce
Mixed Green
50th Star Fruit

Desserts

Cherries Jubilee
Macadamia Nut Ice Cream
Fortune Cookies
Hawaiian Coconut Cake
Guava Sherbet
Banana Souffle, Jamaica Rum Sauce
Beachcomber Delight

Cheese

Edam
Gouda
Gorgonzola
Camembert
Gruyere

Beverages

Coffee
Milk
Sanka
Kona Coffee
Chocolate
Green or Orange Pekoe Tea

BAVARIAN NIGHT

On Bavarian Night, the *Lurline*'s personnel donned Tyrolean costumes and attended the passengers with hearty hospitality. Bavarian décor transformed the marine veranda into a Rathskeller, and strolling musicians serenaded passengers who sipped on beer, compliments of Matson. An old-style Bavarian menu offered *Schnitzel Holstein mit Ei* (breaded veal cutlet, fried egg, lemon, anchovies, and capers) and *Hassenpfeffer auf Deutsche Art* (braised hare with duchess potatoes), as well as luscious German chocolate cake. Their appetites sated, diners proceeded to the Mad Hatter parade and Viennese waltzing contest.

Bavarian Night activities brought broad smiles to the faces of Tiny Berg (hoisting a stein of beer) and, left to right behind him, Mae Brown, Bridgett Messer, and Marsha Haynes.

FIESTA NIGHT

Fiesta Night brought the color and gaiety of Latin America to the S.S. *Lurline*. At cocktail time, passengers spun the Wheel of Fortune to determine the price of their drinks—from free to fifty-five cents—then danced through the cocktail hour. Matson personnel in bright costumes served tempting Spanish entrées—*gallina a la plaza* (fried chicken in green chile sauce) and Mexican red snapper—followed by the mysterious-sounding dessert, *coupe diable rose* (ice cream sundae). The ship's orchestra provided Latin rhythms for dancing on this last night at sea.

In addition to the program of theme night entertainment, an onboard exhibit was organized so that passengers could display souvenirs they had bought on the island. One passenger recalled, "There was everything from shawls and *haoris* to calabashes and *taro* flour, and it was no end of fun."

Fiesta Night menu.

Captain's Dinner and Homecoming Ball

A memorable and elegant occasion, the Captain's Dinner and Homecoming Ball was touched with a hint of *auld lang syne*. Elegant menu selections such as breast of pheasant with truffle sauce or filet mignon with sauce Bordelaise were followed by a dramatic and unforgettable presentation of Matson's Baked Alaska. *Lurline* personnel entertained with their own revue, occasionally interrupted for a performance by a well-known entertainer. Dancing rounded out this glamorous evening.

Matson coffee server.

Baked Alaska ★

Baked Alaska holds a prominent place among the best-loved desserts of all time. Aboard the *Lurline,* it was a hands-down favorite. The dining salon lights were dimmed and in came a host of waiters, bearing the desserts aloft with candles aflame.

SERVES 8 TO 10

2 dozen whole fresh strawberries
1/4 cup curaçao
8 to 10 tablespoons kirsch
Homemade or purchased pound cake, split in half horizontally to form two layers
6 to 8 small scoops of top-quality vanilla ice cream
4 egg whites
1 teaspoon vanilla extract
3/4 cup sugar

Place rack in lower third of oven and preheat to 400°.

Hull strawberries and place in medium bowl. Pour curaçao and 1/4 cup of the kirsch over the top, toss gently, and set aside to marinate.

Place one layer of pound cake on an ovenproof platter suitable for presentation at the table and sprinkle the cake lightly with the remaining kirsch. Cut the remaining layer into slices about 3/8 inch thick.

Arrange scoops of ice cream on top of the bottom cake layer, filling the spaces between scoops with about half of the marinated strawberries. Arrange reserved cake slices on top (using as many as necessary to cover the "layer" of ice cream). Place in the freezer briefly while you prepare the meringue.

Beat egg whites until almost stiff, then gradually add vanilla and sugar. Continue beating just until stiff peaks form.

Remove assembled cake from the freezer. Working quickly, spread meringue over the entire surface, turning a spoon or spatula in the

meringue to create a nice swirled effect. Or place part of the meringue in a pastry bag and pipe rosettes or other shapes onto the surface.

Place the dessert in the oven for approximately 8 minutes. Check frequently, baking just long enough to turn the meringue a pale golden brown. Serve immediately with much fanfare.

Baked Alaska, presented in signature *Lurline* style.

MATSON MEMORABILIA

The souvenir-gathering hadn't ended on the island. Many valuable items in the treasure troves of *Lurline*'s homebound passengers came directly from the ship. The voyage home was the travelers' last chance to gather mementos. Matson provided lots of possibilities for the collector.

Lurline postcards, brochures, and passenger lists were among the most widely collected keepsakes. The beautiful menu covers often were framed and hung, or have survived in scrapbooks and drawers; in either case, they have been and will continue to be handed down from generation to generation.

> They came by ship, excited by dreams of palm trees, white sand beaches, and *hula* maidens. And they returned, their trunks laden with treasures and heads filled with rich stories.
> —Moana Surfrider press kit

OLYNESIAN
A MAGAZINE-A-DAY AT SEA

BY *Matson Line* ☆ VOLUME 1. NUMBER 2 · CALIFORNIA TO

"Mid-Pacific Playground".... All in a Day
Down the Fairway .. On the Wind's Wing
To the Song of the Surf . Where the Big O

Waikiki Sailing

MATSON NAVIGATION COMPANY . . . Hawaii :: South Seas :: Australia

Tasty Lurline Treats

TWO SPECIAL FAVORITES
BY CHEF JERONIMO J. ROMERO

Jeronimo J. Romero, Executive Chef on the Matson Navigation Company's luxury
the S. S. LURLINE, was born in Buenos Aires, Argentina where he served his app
ship. During the First World War, he was in the Argentine Navy and upon dischar
moved to New York City and worked in various hotels and restaurants including
Carlton Terrace, the Endicot Hotel and the Marseilles Hotel.
In 1920, Chef Romero returned to the sea and served on various Trans-Atlantic l
as Sauce Cook. He was promoted to Chef while serving on Panama Pacific Lines' c
ships and stayed with them until 1935.
The Matson Navigation Company, learning of the ability of this rising young sta
the culinary field, engaged Mr. Romero as Sauce Cook on the S. S. Matsonia in 1935.
quickly made Chef and has sailed with the Matson Company since as Chef on several
of their famous luxury liners. In 1952, he was placed in charge of the culinary departme
of the LURLINE and has remained there. Chef Romero has developed a large number
recipes which have tickled the palates of gourmet-minded passengers. We are happy
point two of them so you may try them at home.

CHEESE BLINTZES

pound cottage cheese	1 pound pastry flour
tablespoons brown sugar	3 eggs
teaspoon cinnamon	1 pint milk
orange peel	½ cup butter

the brown sugar and cinnamon together. Strain through a fine strainer.
the orange peel fine and add to the foregoing mixture.
the eggs, flour, milk and butter into a batter. Make into a thin six-inch pancake and
fry until firm but not brown.
the cottage cheese mix in the pancake and fold securely.
butter until golden brown.
with sour cream and strawberry jam. Yield: 16.

CHICKEN LURLINE

ur 3 to 3½ pound chick
oach for five minutes
te wine and juice

Matson Lines

TO HAWAII AND THE SOUTH PACIFIC

Sewing Kit

South Seas
and AUSTRALIA
via HAWAII

The OCEANIC
STEAMSHIP COMPANY
Matson Navigation Co.
Owners and Operators

HAWAIIAN GUIDE
NO. 2

HAWAIIAN ISLANDS

A Handy
BOOK OF
FACTS
about
HAWAII

ISSUED BY THE MATSON NAVIGATION COMPANY

MATSON
presents
EXCITING ON-THE-SPOT REC
HAWAII, "BOAT DAY"—ARRIVAL AND DEPARTURE
"KEEP YOUR EYES ON THE HANDS"—ALFRED APAKA

SELECTIONS
FROM
WEBLEY EDWARDS
"ISLAND
PARADISE"
A
CAPITOL ALBUM
(S)TAO-1229

137

LAST CALL

Steaming to Honolulu was a once-in-a-lifetime experience for many of the thousands and thousands of people who traveled aboard the S.S. *Lurline*. For others, it was one of many such trips. But for everyone, the final night—the last party, the last dinner, the last dance—was especially poignant, as was the following morning.

> The night before we docked back home in San Francisco was an especially fun evening. . . . Hearing the band's rendition of "San Francisco, Open Your Golden Gates" and "California, Here I Come" brought many of us to our feet. At this point it was great to be coming home! Early in the morning before the ship docked, I ventured out onto the deck. I felt something I had not felt for a year: my nose was cold. I was, indeed, home.
>
> —*Margaret Enas*

The coast was now before them, and the islands far behind. Bags were packed and in the early morning light passengers took up places along the railings as the venerable *Lurline* advanced toward her home port. The great ship steamed under the Golden Gate Bridge on the final leg of the bittersweet voyage, and now it was the great city of San Francisco that beckoned to them, welcomed them down the gangplank and back to the arms of the loved ones who awaited them, eager for tales of their adventure across the ocean to paradise.

Louis Melson, chief steward's yeoman, 1933.

GLOSSARY

aloha: welcome, farewell

'awapuhi: native ginger plant

halau: school

haori: short kimono

haupia: coconut pudding

holoku: long dress

hukilau: fishing festival

hula: graceful story-telling dance

imu: pit

kahili: cylinder-shaped feather standard

kalua: bake, baked

kama'aina: native Hawaiian

kane: man

kapu: taboo

keiki: child

koa: a tree (Acacia koa) whose wood is used to create bowls, furniture, surfboards, etc.

kope: coffee

lau hala: pandanus leaf; often plaited to create crafts.

lanai: porch, veranda

laulau: fish, pork, and taro leaves steamed in a ti leaf pouch

le'ale'a: to have fun

liko: newly opened leaf

limu: seaweed

lomilomi: salted salmon, finely diced with tomatoes and onions (lomi translates literally to "massage")

luau: feast

mahimahi: dolphinfish (not dolphin!)

mahalo: thank you (Mahalo nui loa means "Thank you very much.")

makahiki: annual, yearly. (Makahiki Hou means "New Year.")

malihini: newcomer

mele: long poems or songs that convey history and folklore

moe'uhane: dream

moana: broad expanse of ocean

muumuu: loose dress, usually in a bright print fabric

palapala: certificates

poi: ground (or pounded) taro root

taro: a nutritious root

uala: sweet potato

ukulele: "jumping flea"; a small string instrument introduced to the Hawaiian islands by the Portuguese

wahine: woman, lady

wauke: paper mulberry tree

Hawaiian Pronunciation ★

The Hawaiian alphabet contains only twelve letters:

Vowels
a, as in father
e, as in obey
i, as in pique
o, as in vote
u, as in rule

Consonants
h, k, l, m, n, p, and w

The 'okina (or glottal stop—the break between vowels heard in "uh-oh") can be considered a thirteenth letter.

All words and syllables in Hawaiian speech end in vowels, accounting for the language's soft and mellow sounds.

BIBLIOGRAPHY

Aloha Magazine. San Francisco: Matson Navigation Company. May, July, and November 1927.

"Answering the Call: Matson's Fleet at War." *Ampersand* (winter 1991): 3–24.

Bennett, Victor. *Around the World in the Salad Bowl*. San Francisco: Hesperian House, 1961.

Berger, John. "Royal Hawaiian Band Plays On." *Honolulu Star-Bulletin*, 13 April 1999.

Clark, Sydney A. *Hawaii*. New York: Prentice-Hall, Inc., 1939.

Cohen, Stan. *The First Lady of Waikiki: A Pictorial History of the Sheraton Moana Surfrider*. Missoula, Montana: Pictorial Histories Publishing Company, 1995.

———. *The Pink Palace*. Missoula, Montana: Pictorial Histories Publishing Company, 1986.

Delaplane, Stanton. *Postcards from Delaplane*. Garden City, New York: Doubleday & Company, Inc., 1953.

Ferguson, Erna. *Our Hawaii*. New York: Alfred A. Knopf, 1944.

Franzen, David, and Don Hibbard. *The View from Diamond Head: Royal Residence to Urban Resort*. Honolulu: Editions Limited, 1986.

Guest Informant. Los Angeles: Pacific Hotel Publications, Inc., 1962.

Hawaii Visitors and Convention Bureau. "What Is the Hawaii Visitors and Convention Bureau?" 1997 [Online] <www.visit.hawaii.org/hokeo/hvcb/about.html>.

Hommon, Rebecca. "Amelia Earhart: 'First Lady' of the Air and Ford Island." *Hawaii Navy News*, 31 March 2000.

Kam, Nadine. "Boat Days Remembered: Recalling the Golden Days of Steamship Travel to Hawaii." *Waikiki Beach Press*, 6–12 August 1984.

MacDonald, Alexander. *Revolt in Paradise*. New York: Stephen Daye Press, Inc., 1946.

Macfarlane, Richard M. "Lurline off for Hawaii Again." *San Francisco News*, 17 April 1948.

Matson Navigation Company. *Ships in Gray: The Story of Matson in World War II*. San Francisco: Matson Navigation Company, 1946.

———. *Where to Go, What to See, How to Get There, Honolulu*. San Francisco: Matson Navigation Company, 1946.

Old Salt. *The Bon Voyage Book*. New York: The John Day Co., 1931.

Savage, Eugene. Letter to the Palette & Chisel Club, 5 March 1913. *The Cowbell*, the Palette & Chisel Club Newsletter, 1 April 1913.

Sewell, William. "A Matson Purser Recalls 'Boat Days.'" *Honolulu Advertiser*, 14 August 1994.

Stindt, Fred A. *Matson's Century of Ships*. Modesto, California: Privately published, 1982.

Tatar, Elizabeth. *Strains of Change: The Impact of Tourism on Hawaiian Music*. Honolulu: Bishop Museum Press, 1987.

Taylor, Frank J. "Look! Ma's Dancing the Hula!" *Saturday Evening Post* (September 1954).

Tune, Jerry. "Boat Days Renewed." *Honolulu Star-Bulletin*, 16 April 1998.

Warren, Phyllis. *Roger and I Go to Hawaii*. San Francisco: Matson Navigation Company, n.d.

Worden, William L. *Cargoes: Matson's First Century in the Pacific*. Honolulu: University Press of Hawaii, 1981.

IMAGE CREDITS

All images are from the Matson Navigation Company archives unless otherwise stated.

Foreword

page viii, "Glad to Have You Aboard" advertisement, Lynn Blocker Krantz archives.

page 1, S.S. *Monterey* postcard, courtesy of Jesse Lemic.

page 2, "Matson proudly announces" and "The Islands and the Lands Beyond" advertisements, Lynn Blocker Krantz archives.

Prelude

page 3, Eugene Francis Savage, Yale University News Bureau.

Introduction

page 7, Course of the Matson Liners, Lynn Blocker Krantz archives.

page 8, Postcard of the second *Lurline*, William R. Sewell archives.

page 11, "You'll always be glad" advertisement, Lynn Blocker Krantz archives.

page 12, "Hawaii via Matson Lines" advertisement, Lynn Blocker Krantz archives.

page 15, "A new world awaits you" advertisement, Lynn Blocker Krantz archives.

page 17, Postcard of the fourth *Lurline*, William R. Sewell archives.

Bon Voyage

page 20, Margaret Enas photo, courtesy of Margaret Enas; "Sailing Day" advertisement, Lynn Blocker Krantz archives.

page 22, Stationery items, Lynn Blocker Krantz archives.

page 24, Postcard of *Lurline* passing under Golden Gate Bridge, William R. Sewell archives.

page 25, "Nowhere but in the South Seas" advertisement, Lynn Blocker Krantz archives.

page 27, Auto shipping papers, Lynn Blocker Krantz archives.

pages 28–29, Luggage tags, Matson Navigation Company archives and Lynn Blocker Krantz archives.

page 32, Dining table assignment card, Lynn Blocker Krantz archives.

page 33, "At Sea" letter, Lynn Blocker Krantz archives.

page 34, "Thrill to Remember Always" advertisement, Lynn Blocker Krantz archives.

page 36, Table setting, Hawai'i Maritime Center, photo by David Franzen.

page 37, Steward staff photo, courtesy of Louis Melson.

page 38, Mickey Rooney photo, courtesy of Jesse Lemic.

page 39, Beverly Lake photo, courtesy of Beverly Keith.

Fun and Frolic at Sea

page 46, Salad preparation, photo by Carl Zuber.

page 48, Race card, Mary Thiele Fobian archives.

page 49, "On the Sea" letter, Lynn Blocker Krantz archives.

page 51, Message in a bottle, *The Honolulu Advertiser*.

page 52, Shirley Temple photo, courtesy of Jesse Lemic.

page 53, Champagne glass, photo by David Franzen.

page 55, Captain's Dinner menu, Lynn Blocker Krantz archives.

page 56, Matson flag, Lynn Blocker Krantz archives; diners seated at table, William R. Sewell archives.

page 57, Wine steward pouring champagne, courtesy of Jesse Lemic; ice cream server, photo by David Franzen.

Goodbye, Honolulu

ACKNOWLEDGMENTS

Writing this book has been rewarding, interesting, and lots of fun. We've enjoyed conversations and correspondence with many wonderful people we wouldn't otherwise have met.

Special thanks to our collective children—Michael and Kate Krantz, and Anna, Peter, and Max Fobian—for their patience, irrepressible humor, and "down-to-earthness."

And where would we be if it weren't for Larry Fobian's support, encouragement, and technical advice (computer A won't talk to computer B)?

We share our pleasure in this book with everyone who reads it, and to those of you whose names are listed above and below, we say, "Mahalo nui loa!"

Dolores (Mrs. Jack) Abramson
DeeDee Acosta, Hamilton Library,
    University of Hawai'i
Charlene Ahn
Art and Betty Ashfield
Elizabeth Ballentyne
Bob and Lorraine Baxter
Mr. and Mrs. John V. Beahrs
Patty Belchner, Bishop Museum
Tony Bissen, Historian,
    Sheraton Moana Surfrider Hotel
Donald W. Blocker
Betty Britt
Burl Burlingame
Captain John Concannon
Judy Cornell
Covington Public Library,
    Covington, Indiana
Scott Cross, Oshkosh Public Museum
Daniel Delbrel, Executive Chef,
    Sheraton Moana Surfrider Hotel
Martin and June Denny
Sharon Dolan
Eddie Doty
Kirk Driscoll
Margaret Enas
Allan Evenas
Jim and Marian Faber
Doreen Ferritto
G. Fiducia
Cindi and Bob Flating

David Franzen
Mickey Goldsen
Barbara A. Goss
Barbara Gushrowski, Indianapolis
    Museum of Art
Marsha Haynes
Marianne Mike Headley
Frank Hensley, Historian, the Palette &
    Chisel Academy
Lillian Hind
Jeff Hull, Manager, Public Relations,
    Matson Navigation Company
Janet Jarvits
James N. Jensen
Lorena Jones, Ten Speed Press
Beverly Keith
Ken Kouiman, San Francisco
    Maritime Museum
David LaKay
Jesse Lemic
Lorraine and Allan Long
Erica A. MacGuyer, Director of
    Public Relations, Sheraton Moana
    Surfrider Hotel
Ann Malokas
Rene Mansho, Honolulu City
    Council Member
Betty and Willie Marshall
Derrick Mau, Sheraton Moana
    Surfrider Hotel
Joan (Mrs. Robert) McKenzie

Louis F. Melson
Judge Gordon Minder
Ruth (Mrs. Allen) Mitchell
Rudolph and Carlyle Monte
Robert L. Moore, General Manager,
    Hawai'i Maritime Center,
    Honolulu
Chris Pali
Jonathan Parry, Director of Design/
    Merchandising, Homer Laughlin
    China Co.
Gabrielle Pratto
Robert Richardson
Lori Rolander
Earl Rollar
William R. Sewell
Ursula Soares
Captain James M. Stafford
Paul E. Stevens, Senior Vice President,
    Matson Navigation Company
Betsy Stromberg, Designer,
    Ten Speed Press
Kathleen Sullivan
Shirley A. Thomasson
Scott Walls
Holly Taines White, Senior Editor,
    Ten Speed Press
B. J. Whitman, Director of Public
    Relations, Royal Hawaiian Hotel
Philip Wood, Ten Speed Press

INDEX